Praise for
A Life in Letters

"Ronda Beaman has done something extraordinary—she's turned the lost art of letter writing into a bold act of connection, courage, and creativity. *A Life in Letters* doesn't just hit the heart; it hits like a backbeat: honest, raw, and impossible to ignore. As a drummer, I communicate impact and feeling—and Ronda brings both in every line. This book is part memoir, part movement, and all soul. Write on!"

—**Mark Schulman,** drummer for P!NK
and author of *Conquering Life's Stage Fright*

"This book is a handwritten hug, a powerful reminder that the stories we carry—and the ones we dare to write—have the power to change lives, starting with our own. Ronda's letters are raw, brilliant, and unforgettable. It's not just a book; it's a call to reconnect, reclaim your voice, and pick up a pen."

—**Courtney Bonzi,** CEO and founder, Spark*l Bands

"*A Life in Letters* reminds us that true vision isn't about what we see with our eyes, but how we choose to see the world with our hearts. These letters illuminate the courage, humor, and love it takes to navigate life's peaks and valleys—and they encourage all of us to keep climbing toward connection and meaning."

—**Erik Weihenmayer,** athlete, adventurer, and author of *No Barriers*

"*A Life in Letters* is a beautiful, bold invitation to slow down and reconnect—with yourself, with others, and with the power of your own voice. Ronda Beaman writes with such vulnerability and wit that it's impossible not to be moved—and inspired. As an advocate of sustainable living, I deeply value the tactile, lasting nature of handwritten connection. This book is a reminder that what we write, and how we love, can truly leave a legacy."

—**Nicola Reed,** cofounder of Beeble

"I felt privileged to read such a private letter journal because of the personal and sometimes profound words. I appreciate the depth and scope of her writing due to Ronda's attention to subtleties in relationships. I enjoyed learning from *A Life in Letters*."

—**Inga Buccella,** *Readers' Favorite* review

"*A Life in Letters* is more than a memoir. It's a master class in vulnerability, legacy, and the courage it takes to put pen to paper. These letters remind us that it's never too late to say what matters."

—**Jonathan Koch,** Emmy Award–winning producer

"This soulful wake-up call is chockablock stuffed with AI—authentic inspiration—to reflect, express, and connect in the most gorgeously simple and potent way: through the simple act of writing a letter."

—**Paul G. Stoltz,** CEO, PEAK Learning, Inc.

"*A Life in Letters* reminds readers that writing and sending a letter is like giving the recipient a gold medal. It will be saved, treasured, and shared, and your efforts will be rewarded."

—**Christopher Blevins,** Olympic, world,
and Pan-American mountain-biking champion

"Hospitality is about creating connections that last well beyond a single moment. In *A Life in Letters*, Ronda Beaman extends that same spirit—welcoming us into stories that remind us of our shared humanity, our responsibility to one another, and the enduring power of kindness."

—**Wolfgang M. Neumann,** global hospitality leader
and sustainability advocate

"Ronda's words invite us to embrace vulnerability, celebrate resilience, and lead with courage from wherever we are."

—**Kiah Twisselman Burchett,** speaker, coach,
and women's leadership advocate

A Life in Letters

Also by the Author

Student Development and College Teaching
You're Only Young Twice
Little Miss Merit Badge
Seal with a Kiss
My Feats in These Shoes

A Life in Letters

Notes and Prompts for a Return to Pen and Paper

DR. RONDA BEAMAN

amplify
an imprint of Amplify Publishing Group

www.amplifypublishing.com

A Life in Letters: Notes and Prompts for a Return to Pen and Paper

For more information, please contact:
Amplify Publishing, an imprint of Amplify Publishing Group
620 Herndon Parkway, Suite 220
Herndon, VA 20170
info@amplifypublishing.com

Library of Congress Cataloging-in-Publication Data has been applied for.

CPSIA Code: PRV1125A

ISBN-13: 979-8-89138-922-9

Printed in the United States

For Paul.

Because one letter changed everything.

I remain,

Very Truly Yours.

Contents

RECEIVED
Ans'd
By
A 23
POSTAGE

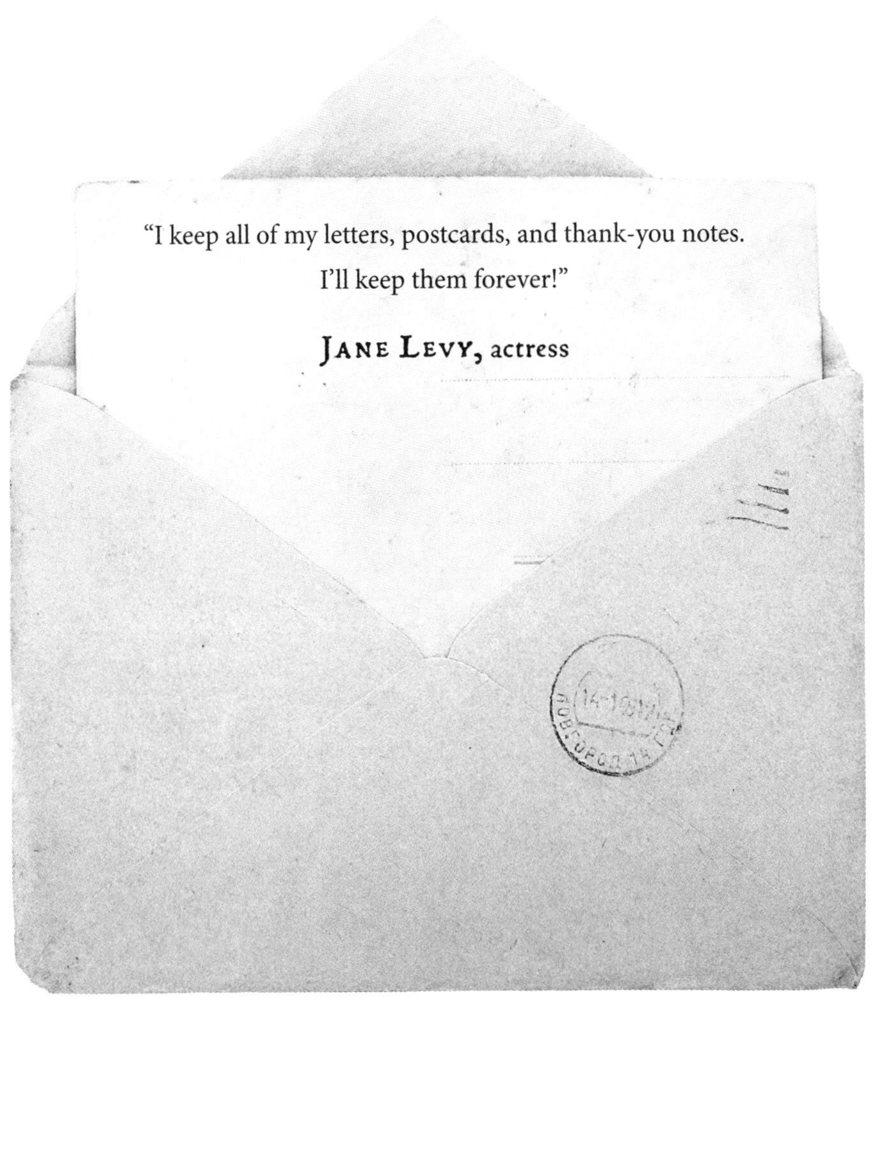
"I keep all of my letters, postcards, and thank-you notes.
I'll keep them forever!"
Jane Levy, actress

SPECIAL DELIVERY

BY AIR MAIL
PAR AVION

BY AIR MAIL
PAR AVION

Dear Reader

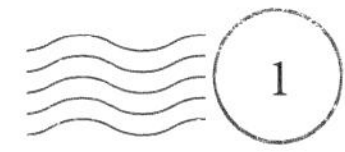

"A letter should be regarded not merely as a medium for the communication of intelligence," an 1876 book of etiquette stated, "but also as a work of art."

This art form has become all too rare in a world that's forgotten its magic. This book isn't just a collection of my letters; it's an invitation to rediscover the power of words written by hand, with care and intention.

Letter writing is more than communication—it's connection, reflection, and sometimes even transformation. A letter is a piece of yourself, preserved in ink and paper, that says, "I cared enough to take the time." In an age of fleeting texts and endless notifications, letters offer something priceless: permanence and presence.

The letters in this book are raw, honest, and deeply human. They capture the joy, regret, gratitude, and humor of life—emotions we all feel but often leave unsaid.

The idea for this book came from an article I read about Swedish death cleaning. The main point was to clear out your stuff before your kids have to do it when you die. This scared me, not because of dying, but because I wasn't sure what was in those boxes that I might not want my sons to see. So I unpacked boxes and hope chests and lockers and files of memorabilia from my life and came to terms with what was junk, essential, or dubiously neither. Out went unflattering photos of me, which cut the collection of mementos from thousands to hundreds. Goodbye to dried corsages from proms of the past; so long to cocktail napkins, pilfered menus, and swizzle sticks from distant dates, as well as mothball-resistant cheerleading sweaters, swim team ribbons, and even high school yearbooks signed by friends for life . . . that I never saw again after they signed "2Good2Bforgotten."

This eviction of my life's evidence was distressing and depressing to be sure—"Is that all there is?" as the song goes. However, as though I were sifting through the ashes after a house burned down, hoping to find an heirloom or spared remnant of meaning and mattering, I held on to, read every word of, and wrapped in ribbon the letters I received from friends, family, teachers, grade school pen pals, lovers, and other notable characters in my life. Some torrid, some terrible or funny, some so delicately worded and heartfelt they brought me to tears. Some so funny or cute I laughed out loud. Letters that were twelve pages long, one line, or just a symbol, like when I asked my dad why he never wrote me a note while I was in college and he mailed me this:

Love, Daddy

These letters were worth saving. I couldn't bring myself to throw them in the trash. The handwriting, in particular, stirred me. It revealed quirks, flourishes, and tiny imperfections that reflected the writer's personality. It's as if a piece of the person is embedded in the letter. Their name signed at the bottom gave me a pang of remembrance, gratitude, and sheer joy. Love letters took me back to a time in life when I was a completely different person. Camp letters from my children reminded me who they were and how similar they are to the grown-ups they've become. To see my grandmother's wingding capital letters or my brother's tiny, perfect printing was to harken back to the time before they both died. Clever handmade cards from my sister displayed her abundant talent before that talent was diluted by alcohol.

Thirty-four years ago, it was a carefully crafted Magna Carta of a letter that

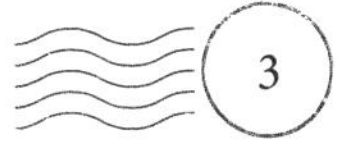

my husband wrote to me that catapulted our relationship to marriage in less than a year.

The letters from my mother-in-law still smell of cigarettes. My college roommate's coffee-stained missives, or my boyfriend's letters—typed on railroad notepads the summer he worked for Union Pacific—are all time capsules telling my life story and those of the characters in it. Rummaging through the letters I kept made me wonder if someone had kept a letter I wrote, which then progressed to the notion of figuring out whom I owe a letter and why.

A Life in Letters is therefore filled with letters I should have written but didn't. It's a one-way correspondence of sentiments I should have shared, stories I ought to have told, and forgiveness I withheld.

Author Philip Roth called the unsent letter "a flourishing subliterary genre with a long and moving history." For biographer Janet Malcom, letters were "fossils of feeling" that become emotional banks of what and how we once felt and put a finger to the pulse of a moment in our lives when we throbbed with emotion. My hope is that these examples will inspire you to write your own letters—whether it's to express something you've never had the courage to say, to reconnect with someone you've drifted from, or simply to reflect on your life. Throughout this process I have discovered that writing letters can bring clarity, healing, and even unexpected joy. Letter writing can also be a life-review process and is certainly more pleasant than Swedish death cleaning. I also believe that writing these letters has saved me thousands of dollars in therapy.

Some of these letters were scribbled in haste, some in tearful reminiscence. As Emily Dickinson wrote in her unsent love letters, "It is finished can never be said of us." And there is, truthfully, nothing finished about our lives, our loves, or our letters.

I hope you use *A Life in Letters* as a guide, a nudge, or a creative spark. Let it remind you that your words matter, your voice deserves to be heard, and your thoughts are worth preserving.

Ultimately, writing letters like this can become both a personal release and a gift to others—a record of the complex, beautiful, and sometimes bittersweet connections that shape our lives.

People are hungry for a personal touch. Day by day we become physically separated bit by bit from the world. Now is the time to put down your phone and pick up a pen.

Imagine this: your words, in your handwriting. No filters, no autocorrect—just your thoughts, your heart, and the pen in your hand.

Take a moment to slow down and fill a blank page with your personality. Share a memory, write a thank-you, or say what you've always wanted to say. Each word, each line will be a tiny piece of you—ink that can't be deleted and smudges that speak of your touch. It's something the recipient can hold, reread, and keep, long after the texts have faded away.

Even if, like my first-grade teacher, the person you write to will never see your letter, it's a gesture, a gift, and a little piece of your heart, all wrapped up in paper and ink. It's your art.

My wish is that after sharing my letters with you, you will share yours, to send or to heal. Poet Donald Hall said in an interview in *The Paris Review* that "Letters are my society, my café, my club, my city."

So find a piece of paper and start writing. Holding the paper, noticing the texture, even smelling the ink or paper can evoke deep emotional responses. As your pen moves, you are tracing lines of your life onto paper. The mere act of writing is an exercise in immense patience and reclaiming focus in a highly distracting world.

By writing letters, you'll not only connect with others in a more meaningful way but also connect with yourself. And who knows? If you send your letter, you might get one back. This could be the start of a letter-writing renaissance.

With pen in hand,

Ronda

San Luis Obispo, California

2025

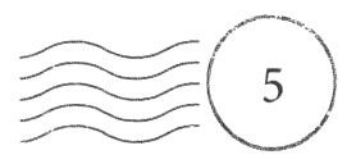

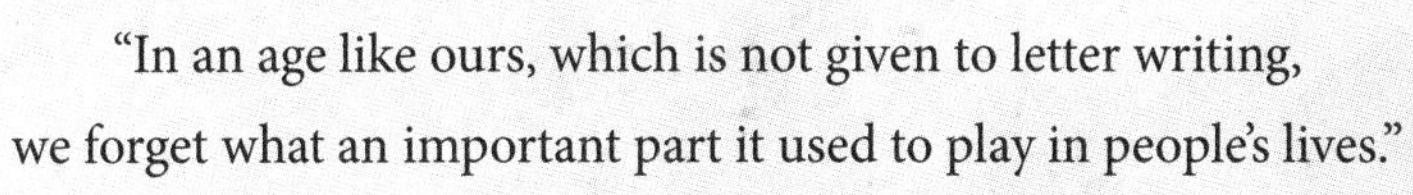

"In an age like ours, which is not given to letter writing,
we forget what an important part it used to play in people's lives."

Anatole Broyard

Dear Writer

A Life in Letters is a collection of letters I wish I had sent, shared to inspire you to do the same.

You may not write to your first-grade teacher like I did, but there's a letter waiting to be written to someone who taught you, coached you, believed in you—or didn't. Writing these letters encourages introspection. You may find yourself better understanding past situations and your reactions to them, which can foster self-awareness. Through this process, you gain insight into your own behaviors, which can be empowering and even transformative. My letters became a sort of cathartic memoir. Apologizing, explaining, or expressing gratitude allows you to release feelings that might have been building up over time. Whether or not you send the letter, just putting your thoughts on paper can provide closure and alleviate mental burdens.

Here is the process I used to write my letters. It's just an expanded version of what our mothers told us to do when we sent thank-you notes for our birthday gifts or graduation money.

- **Know Your Purpose:** Be clear about why you're writing and whom you're writing to. Whether it's a thank-you note, an apology, a love letter, or just a means of catching up, understanding the purpose will help you focus and make the message more heartfelt.
- **Start with a Thoughtful Opening:** Rather than jumping straight into the topic, ease in with a warm greeting. A personal opening, like recalling a shared memory or acknowledging the last time you connected, can set a friendly, inviting tone.
- **Be Sincere and Personal:** Write as if you're speaking directly to the person, using your natural voice. Personalize it with details or anecdotes that are meaningful to your relationship; this will make the letter feel unique and genuine.
- **Pay Attention to Structure:** Think of your letter like a conversation with a beginning, middle, and end. Start by introducing your thoughts, delve into the main message, and then wrap up with a closing thought. This

gives the letter a smooth flow.

- **Use Concrete Details:** Add specific details to make your words more vivid. Instead of making general statements, tell them about particular moments, places, or feelings. These details can create a more memorable, evocative letter.
- **Keep It Positive and Kind:** Even if you're addressing something difficult, approach it with warmth and kindness. Letters often become keepsakes, and they'll be read and reread, so try to convey empathy and understanding.
- **End on a Thoughtful Note:** Close with something that leaves a positive impression. A closing remark could be a well-wish, an expression of gratitude, or a hint at future plans. It helps the recipient feel connected to you even after the letter ends.
- **Write Legibly and Presentably:** Since I am urging you to write a handwritten letter, write clearly and carefully—slowing down can also make the experience more intentional. Choosing good paper and a favorite pen can add a touch of elegance and care.
- **Reread Before Sealing:** Take a moment to read over what you've written. It's easy to miss typos or unclear parts in the flow of writing, and this small check can ensure your message comes across as you intend.
- **Allow for Imperfection:** Don't worry about making it flawless. Part of what makes a letter endearing is its authenticity—even small imperfections, like crossed-out words or little smudges, remind the reader that it was written by hand, just for them.

If you focus on sincerity, personal connection, and thoughtful presentation, your letter will likely feel special and genuine—something the recipient may treasure long after they read it.

You will find a blank page after each of my letters. I challenge you to strike while the pen is hot and write a note to someone you thought of while reading mine. Then tear it out and keep it, send it, or burn it. There is enchantment in writing a letter, and someone, somewhere, wants one from you.

Grab a pen, a piece of paper, and begin.

Ronda

Good Reasons to Write a Letter

Someone is waiting for a letter from you. Pick one of these reasons, decide who is the recipient, and write now.

1. **Express Gratitude:** A handwritten thank-you note feels more sincere and thoughtful than a quick text or email.
2. **Reconnect with Someone:** Writing to a friend or family member you haven't seen in a while shows that you care enough to take the time.
3. **Celebrate Special Moments:** Send letters for birthdays, anniversaries, or achievements to make the celebration more memorable.
4. **Provide Encouragement:** A supportive note can be a beacon of hope during tough times.
5. **Share Memories:** Letters can capture stories, reflections, or milestones that might otherwise fade over time.
6. **Preserve a Legacy:** Letters often become keepsakes, offering future generations a glimpse into your thoughts and experiences.
7. **Apologize or Mend Relationships:** A heartfelt letter allows you to express your emotions thoughtfully and without interruption.
8. **Practice Mindfulness:** Writing a letter is a slower, intentional act that can help you process your feelings and communicate authentically.

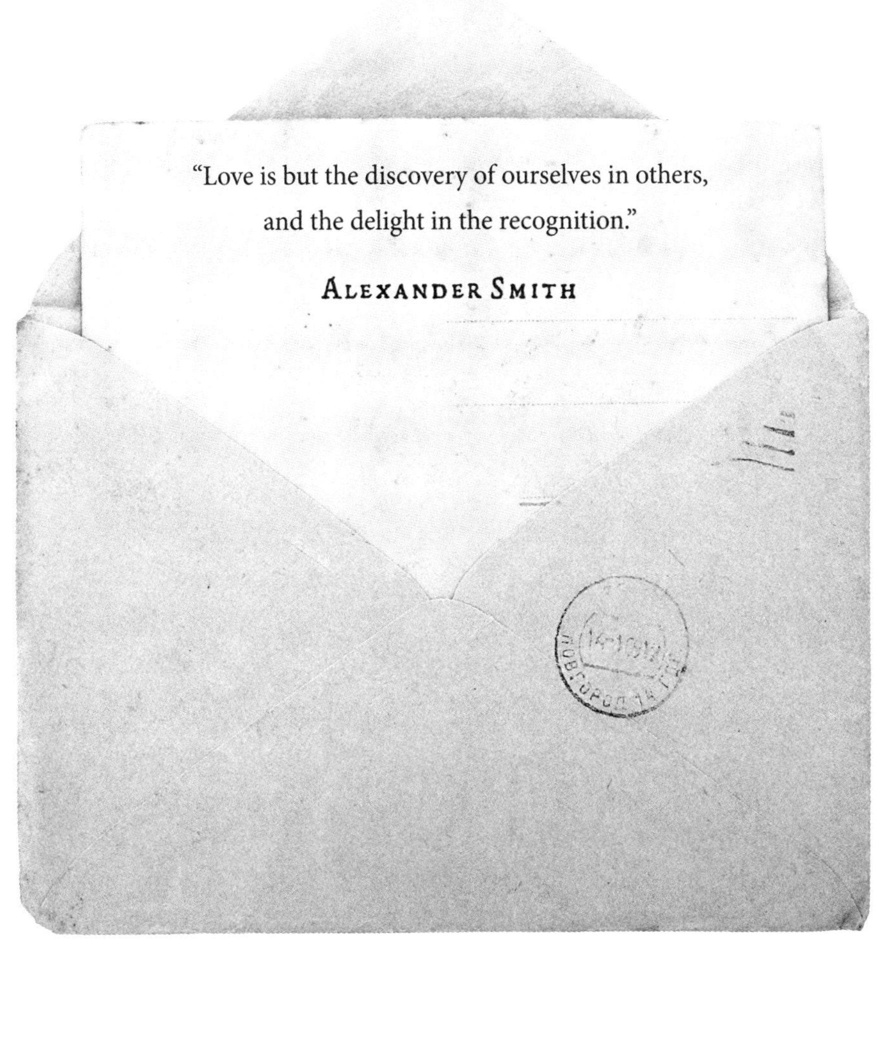

"Love is but the discovery of ourselves in others, and the delight in the recognition."

Alexander Smith

A Letter of Firsts

For my first-grade teacher, Mrs. Pierce,

You had no way of knowing that by the time I walked into your classroom that morning, I had already been in three different first grades, in three different states.

I wore a new dress that day, but I carried old problems—moving too much, parents who were too young, and the unsettled, insecure feeling of always being the new kid.

I don't need to tell you that many children are not especially welcoming, kind, or generous. But thankfully—and to my undying benefit—you were all three.

It was your warm smile, the way you pulled a desk from the back of the room to place beside yours, the way you wrapped me up in the generous, ample bosom of your embrace that let me know I was going to be OK at Orangewood Elementary.

Maybe you knew I needed you. But my suspicion, now that I am a teacher myself, is that you were wonderful and welcoming to every student who passed through your door. And how fortunate I was to be one of them.

You didn't just give me a place to sit—you gave me a place to belong. You didn't just teach me how to read—you showed me how a teacher can change the world with kindness, patience, and a steadfast belief in the child in front of her.

You were my starting block in education, and I completed the run with a PhD.

I dedicate this degree to you and the commencement you gave me.

Forever Pierced,

Ronda

A Letter of Slapstick

Dear Wallace and Ladmo,

I needed to be noticed, I needed to be rewarded, I needed to win your "Ladmo Bag."

I was sitting in the front row of fidgety kids corralled inside the TV station where your daily cartoon show was being filmed. Multiple schools had joined in the field trip to be your audience. As you know, *The Wallace and Ladmo Show* was the highest rated and most watched program in Phoenix. And the annual field trip to the television station to watch you live was more exciting and anticipated than the other field trip favorite, the Wonder Bread tour.

All the kids were screaming your names, waving their hands, jumping up and down so fast and hard the bleachers sounded like one of the summer thunderstorms in Arizona. I remember thinking, "If I sit still and simply smile at you, maybe dare a small knowing wink if we make eye contact, I know you will pick me as the Ladmo Bag winner." I angled my Brownie beanie, dropped my chin a bit, and waited for you to Ladmo me.

Unbelievably, the Ladmo Bag filled with candy, chips, and soda went to two of the loudest yelling kids, waving their hands wildly, who weren't even Scouts. So much for jaunty beanies and furtive smiles.

But I instantly forgave both of you for making this terribly wrong choice because I adored you.

I loved you for making me laugh, for being silly, and for taking life lightly. I loved you for the costumes, cartoons, and conversations you shared with me. And until the day I sat with the live audience of screaming crazies who also loved you, I did believe your show was broadcast just for me.

I needed you. I had already attended three different schools for first grade, lived in multiple houses, and felt the undefined ache so many children have when they aren't treasured at home. *The Wallace and Ladmo Show* became my family by choice every weekday afternoon. I am sure for every day of the thirty-five years you were on the air, for every hour you clowned and cajoled, you were broadcasting love, lessons, and life to thousands of kids. But mostly me.

Did anyone tell you that their childhood was brighter and better because of you? Mine sure was. My teenage parents were busy trying to feed my siblings and me, trying to earn rent and then respite at the ends of long days. They were kids raising kids and not lighthearted cartoon-show hosts like you. Plopping me in front of your show was an escape for my mom and expanding for me. All the skits and characters, the tips and tricks, and your sense of humor and fun filled me with a wider sense of the world—and my place in it. I was not restricted to a little blue brick house in Arizona. I believed I could grow up to be on a show, host cartoons, be funny and kind. If Ladmo was a star, I could be one too.

Thank you from a little girl, in a little living room, sitting in front of a little black-and-white TV, who felt seen while watching you.

The "Ladmo Bag" I did finally get contained a gift bigger and better than candy and chips. I wasn't alone if I spent afternoons with my friends Wallace and Ladmo.

From the Brownie Scout, winking politely and quietly in the front row, seat 15,

Ronda

A Letter of Affection

Principal Bonaco,

Did it seem strange to you that at least once a day I found a reason to come to the principal's office? Most kids dreaded being sent to see you. I, on the other hand, volunteered and commandeered any opportunity to walk down the breezeway at Orangewood Elementary in hopes I might see you. Turning in attendance sheets or permission slips, picking up extra supplies for my teacher, if it got me sent to where you were, I raised my hand.

I had my reasons.

Sure, the suit and tie. You looked like Walter Cronkite on the *CBS Evening News*. Gray at the temples, with black eyeglasses and a deep voice, and when you needed a pen, you pulled one from the pocket inside your jacket. I thought that was so elegant. Your lanky, loose-limbed walk down the sidewalk to visit classrooms, how all my teachers smiled when they saw you.

I looked forward to morning announcements on the PA system, and I think I may have been the only student who got your Johnny Carson joke when the school secretary would say, "Heeeer's Mr. Bonaco!" I would giggle every time and shush kids who were talking. More than once a student sitting close to me asked to be moved away from the girl who had a crush on the principal.

I didn't care. They did not know about the pitter-patter of your little heart.

Each and every time I showed up at the office, upon seeing me you put your right hand inside the left side of your suit and made your jacket move up and down while saying, "Hello, young lady, you look so nice today, you make my little heart go pitter-pat." Then you would smile, escort me to the door, and get back to principaling. I would skip back to class with a bigger smile than when I left it.

You saw me, you paid attention and shared delight, and I felt like I mattered. You, Mr. Bonaco, gave me your heart, and you remain in mine.

Pitter-patter,

Ronda

A Letter of Rhymes

Dear Grandma Echo,

I *ode* you a letter, and since you wrote me so many poems throughout my life, I am returning the favor.

You were a wild woman, a flaming-redheaded kook
Having you as my grandma was clearly no fluke
Like chocolate and peanut butter or toast and jam
We belonged together—you're part of me and who I am
Thirty-six when I arrived, my mother a mere teen
It wasn't a great start, if you know what I mean
You had to be the breadwinner and surrogate mom
You took it all on with style and aplomb

I wonder now, what were your dreams, your hopes and wishes
Did you ever consider being more than a Mrs.?
You were like that poster from World War II
In a scarf with a drill, Uncle Sam wanted you
You carried the burden, and you carried me too
You made sure I survived parents with no clue

Fun, bombastic, a dancing machine
Little did I know you were hooked on morphine
Married multiple times to men who only saw a body
At 40 double D, you have to admit, you were a hottie

The beautiful birthday-skirt cakes surrounding my Barbie doll
We got pierced ears together at a Los Angeles mall
You made my wedding gown, stitch by stitch, pearl by pearl
You called me "Sugar Plum"; I was your special girl

Decades have gone by, but like your name, you return
For one more adventure with you, I consistently yearn
To bake a pie, learn to sew, to do riddles and rhymes
To pop your back blackhead with a bobby pin, those were good times

I'll never see you again on this earth, but in my heart, you remain
It's been said you're not gone if someone utters your name
Echo Rose . . . Echo Rose . . . there will never be another
My life is your Echo, my much-loved grandmother

Your one and only Sugar Plum,
Ronda

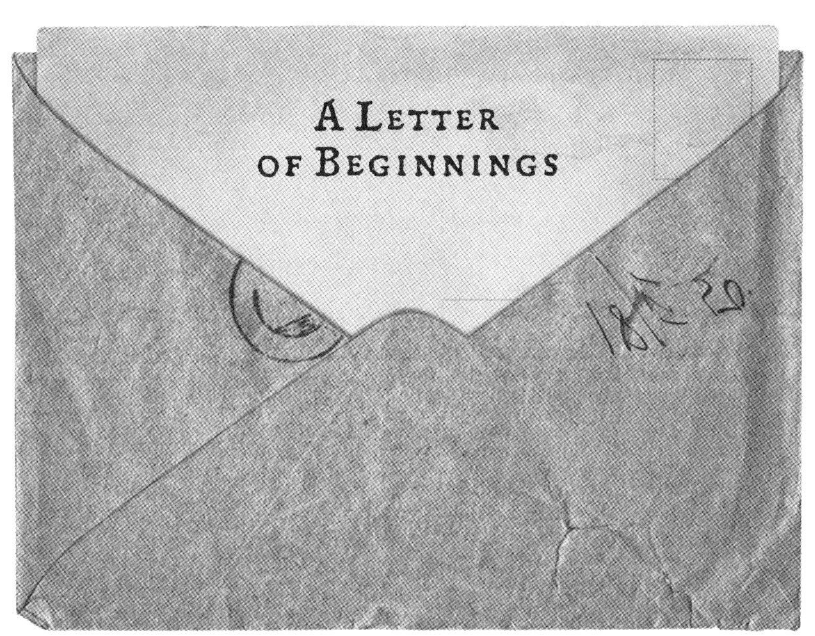

A Letter of Beginnings

Dear Wesley Birch,

I never spoke to you and never played tag or tetherball with you, yet to this day, I remember you from second grade as the exemplar of boys as human beings.

Until I encountered you, boys were a loud, spitting, snotty, always in motion, annoying, hair-pulling, and dusty subspecies related, not even distantly, to the cartoon Tasmanian Devil. Did I mention smelly?

Anyway, one day on the playground, you walked up to me, handed me a dandelion, and smiled. I had never seen dimples until that moment, and I wanted some of my own. Still do. Your hair was parted on the side and combed, your shirt was a brown-and-beige plaid, and you had creased jeans, clean hands, and a flower, for me.

Wherever you are, Wesley Birch from Orangewood Elementary, without a word you spoke volumes. Guys can be kind, caring, cute, and clean . . . and that has been my standard since that day on the playground.

And what if, Wesley Birch? What if like friends of mine who met in the third grade and married after college, sweethearts from the moment they laid eyes on each other, even without dimples, what if you had said something, what if I had answered, and what if . . . well, that is the real story of life, isn't it? The road less taken, or not even started on, the fairy tale, the Prince Charming, the dream. If we had married, had children, mortgages, orthodontics, wrestled through job loss, in-laws, had stayed in hot, now overcrowded Phoenix, would dimples have been enough?

I am glad you remained silent, that I moved from that school shortly after, that I didn't have to share a bathroom with you or get tired of your stories or suffer through the thousands of moments in a lifetime where giving me a flower wouldn't help. Instead, I treasure the memory of a little boy with Brylcreem in his hair, a dandelion in his hand, and a dimpled smile. And occasionally daydream about what might have been.

Dimpleless,

Ronda

A Letter of Soulmates

Dear Packy, in honor of Meme,

The first time I saw you, Packy, you were pure magic. A baby elephant, the first born in the United States in forty-four years, and right there in my grandmother's city—Portland, Oregon. The whole town hummed with excitement, as if you had trumpeted your arrival straight into our hearts. I was just a child myself, my small hand tucked inside Meme's, both of us navigating the sea of visitors at the Oregon Zoo, eager for a glimpse of you.

And there you were—wobbly, wide-eyed, and ears flapping like you hadn't quite figured out what to do with them. A wrinkled bundle of wonder. I pressed my face against the railing, utterly transfixed. Had anything so magnificent ever before existed?

Well, maybe one thing.

My grandmother—my hand-holder, my adventure guide, my firm but loving compass. She was the kind of person who made the world feel safe but never small. That day, she hoisted me onto her hip so I could see you better, laughing as I squealed at your every uncertain step. We counted your tiny freckles, fed peanuts to your mother, and before we left, Meme bought me a stuffed toy version of you—something small enough to carry but big enough to hold the memory of that day.

Fifty years later, I came back to the zoo. Time had changed everything and nothing.

You were massive now, Packy. No longer a baby but a legend, towering and steady, a living monument to time itself. As I stood there staring at you, I felt another presence just as powerfully. Meme. I heard her laughter, saw her shaking her head at the price of zoo admission, felt the warmth of her hand, as if no years had passed at all.

They say elephants never forget. That family is their anchor, their unshakable truth. That love and loyalty are stitched into their very being.

Looking into your eyes, I believed it.

Because in that moment, we weren't just two creatures separated by years and species. We were bound by something deeper—a knowing. A shared understanding that life moves forward, but love holds firm.

I still have that little stuffed version of you. It sits where I can see it, a small but mighty reminder of your baby self and of my beautiful Meme. And every time I look at it, I'm reminded that the best things in life aren't just moments—they're the love we wrap around them.

Thank you, Packy, for growing up alongside my love for her. For standing as proof that some bonds never fade, no matter how many years pass.

With love and a trunk load of memories,

Ronda Ann

A Letter of
Criminal Intent

Oh, Mrs. Lauman,

I don't see any point in holding grudges.

I think that every teacher I had did their level best to help me learn. Some were better than others, and of course, some just connected better with me than others. Teaching is a vital, yet unappreciated and often disrespected, job, and those who do it deserve our thanks for their service, just as the first responders and military veterans do.

All of them . . . except you.

I'm not holding a grudge.

I, 100 percent, hold a deep and abiding loathing.

You stood me up in front of my entire third-grade class and announced that I had stolen the money my parents put in the PTA envelope I delivered that morning. You showed the empty envelope and said, "You should be ashamed."

Not me, Mrs. Lauman, because I didn't steal anything. But you did, Mrs. Lauman. You stole my joy of third grade, my reputation with my classmates, and my respect and regard for you. So as a third grader would say, "Shame, shame, everyone knows your name."

Firstly, I want to assure you that if I were to venture into a life of crime, stealing three dollars of PTA money wouldn't exactly be at the top of my list. Diamonds, maybe. Exotic pets, possibly. But PTA money? Really?

Now, on to the accusation itself. I must commend you on your creative imagination. It takes true genius to frame an innocent student with such finality. Like putting me in front of a firing squad, you delivered your shots and then told me to sit down.

However, if I were to commit such a crime, I would have left behind an envelope of glitter and confetti as my signature; I like getting credit.

The envelope your squinty-eyed self was so sure contained the missing funds was handed to me by my parents that morning, who, I can assure you, were not running a sophisticated embezzlement operation from our humble home.

Speaking of home, when I returned at the end of the worst school day of my life, I didn't even tell anyone, I was so rattled and mortified. "Did the money drop out?" I wondered. "Did someone else take it after I put it on her desk?"

The next morning, I tried hard to get out of going to school. My mother finally asked, "What is wrong with you? I thought you loved school?"

I told on you, Mrs. Lauman.

My mother was furious; turns out she forgot to put the money in the envelope before I left for school.

The next morning my mother handed me a sealed envelope.

"Give this to your teacher, and it will fix everything," she told me. "It's a letter Daddy wrote last night."

I skipped to school, said jolly hellos to my classmates as I walked up to your desk, and politely said, "My dad asked me to give this to you," and handed you the note. Standing by your desk, watching you as you opened the envelope and began to read it, I was thinking how great it would be to put this all behind us, to remain your pet, and to have my name cleared in front of the class. "Thanks, Daddy," I thought, with imaginary hearts floating above my head.

Those hearts burst as I watched your face begin to turn red, then purple, then squinch until you were unrecognizable. Like cartoons I had seen, steam was escaping from your ears, foam from your mouth, and I could hear high-pitched sounds from deep within your throat.

I found out later that when my dad heard the gory details of your accusation, he wrote a scathing, foul-worded letter to you to blow off some steam. It was never meant to be delivered, but my mother didn't know that. I can't fathom what it might have said, but I can appreciate it must have been unkind, accusatory, nasty, and mean . . . like you.

My dad took the "pen is mightier than the sword" aphorism a bit too literally! You put the letter down, looked up at me, and said, "Now I know where you get it." I wasn't sure what "it" was, but I knew "it" wasn't good. Right there and then, you ordered me to pull all my books and papers out of the front-row desk I had previously occupied and move to a single, desolate, unused desk in the back of the classroom. The other kids either snickered or were stricken by my rapid demotion. And that lone dunce desk was mine for the remainder of third grade. You didn't look at me, call on me, or acknowledge my presence the rest of the year.

I learned some valuable lessons that year that had nothing to do with reading, writing, or arithmetic. If the people you love defend you, if you know you are good and right and true, it doesn't much matter what anyone else, even a teacher, thinks of you. I made it through your miserable class, I didn't let your grinchness make me feel like I was nothing, and I decided I would someday teach and strive to broaden, not diminish; believe, not belittle; and love, not loathe, any student sitting in my classroom.

And I have done that for over thirty-five years.

In conclusion, I want to clarify that I did not steal anything, except maybe a few hearts with my insistent innocence and play-by-play storytelling about the whole event through the years.

Mrs. Lauman, always double-check the evidence before pointing fingers.

Ronda

A Letter of Lies

Dear Brian Wilson,

When "Help me, Rhonda" hit the charts, everyone at Orangewood Elementary was singing it and buying the 45, and I told yet another in a long string of whoppers from my childhood. "Yes," I said, "they wrote it for me. I met all the Beach Boys at a dance party for my dad's work in Palm Springs."

Had I ever been to Palm Springs? No. Had I ever met any Beach Boys? Only in my girlhood dreams. But that didn't stop me from describing how cute Denny the drummer was, or how I was thrilled to be the inspiration for the song. I told classmates that you spelled my name wrong because you wanted to keep our relationship a secret! I was eleven years old.

Look, I am not saying I got away with this, or any of my fictional life. I just so wanted to be somebody. I wanted to be swept away from my real home and reside in the mansion I believed awaited me. And I was impatient. After all, I was already in the sixth grade. You were only sixteen when you started the Beach Boys; I only had four years, I figured, to become something.

I didn't play piano, didn't read music, tried out for chorus and was put in the back row with girls way taller than me who croaked out only a part of each song, but we snapped our fingers while the sopranos sang. I didn't have any training in dance or drama. There was no apparent vehicle, meaning talent, for me to become a superstar, with the exception of falsehood construction and delivery. On this I was masterful.

I admit it, Brian: I had a perverse and pathological need to play in a bigger arena than suburban Phoenix, and saying that "Help me, Rhonda" was all about me was another possible ticket to ride . . . sorry. I think I remember saying Paul McCartney was a pal too.

The one thing I did have working in my favor, besides chutzpah, was a dad who moved us on average every six months. At just about the time my classmates began to catch on to my compulsive fibs, we moved somewhere else, and I could start my identity anew.

I am proud to report to you, Brian, that the "Help Me, Rhonda" story held steady through at least four other schools. It had real staying power. I think it was a combination of earnest storytelling combined with the implausible pick of my name for a song. Using Rhonda, or Ronda, was an unorthodox choice. Valerie, sure. Beth, always popular. But Rhonda, or more correctly, Ronda? Never done before or since. We both got a lot of play from that song. You hit number 1 on *Billboard*, knocking the Beatles off the charts, and helped me, Ronda, establish myself as a legend in a number of elementary schools.

I'm writing to tell you that I eventually made the change from a period as in *Help me. Ronda* to a comma as in "Help me, Ronda." Meaning the song transitioned from a self-aggrandizing mouthpiece intended to deliver friends and morphed into the background music of my mission in life. "Help me, Ronda" has been my motto and has given meaning, purpose, and direction to my life.

By high school, lying had run its course. I wanted to do things that were not only positive and important but believed by real, live people and, most importantly, become someone credible. I ran for school offices and became a creative resource for my teachers: I designed bulletin board competitions between classrooms; produced cassette tape reenactments of history lessons; shot eight-millimeter music videos from the likes of Simon and Garfunkel or the Dave Clark Five (way ahead of MTV); was active in pep club, cheer, girls' club—you name it—if a volunteer was needed, my hand automatically shot up. Thanks to the zeal of my veracity, I garnered awards and accolades and was admitted to a good college. I was the first person in my family to graduate from college, and Brian, your song and the inspiration of it is honestly the reason. If I had kept concocting life instead of composing it, the pitch and refrain of my tale would not be the same.

"Help me, Ronda" has echoed through the chapters of my life. To this day, decades later, whether the person is young, old, or in between, inevitably when I meet someone they say, "Oh, like 'Help Me, Rhonda'?" Your song is not only my raison d'être; it's my ringtone. And when someone calls, it is generally because they need help, guidance, a laugh, some direction in life, or just a friendly voice to remind them that things will get better. And I answer those calls, always bearing in mind that I am here to help.

So thank you, Brian. Your song didn't just top the charts; it helped shape a life. Mine.

No lie,

Ronda

A Letter of Envy

To Pam Keasey, if that's still your name,

You probably married young, had tons of babies, and lost your figure. Or that's my hope.

I am not proud that I am still the jealous, small, petty, gossipy girl I was in the fifth grade. But I am.

I really don't want to know if you married rich, have a personal trainer or tennis coach, and fly around the world lunching with Amal Clooney or sipping champagne before your private chef brings in your dinner.

Sorry, I digress. This apology letter is to confess.

It was me.

I was a "mean girl" before anyone had ever used the phrase. You were my best friend back in the day of playing Barbies and wearing surfer bangs. I truly liked you, but so did everyone else. And oh, how they would torment me by asking, "Is Pam as nice as she seems?" and by saying, "Oh, you are so lucky to be Pam's friend." And the last straw, "Pam is so pretty." "Oh, Pam, she is the most beautiful girl in our school." "Have you ever seen anyone prettier than Pam?"

I couldn't take it. I couldn't bear it. I couldn't stand it. I broke.

Whenever anyone started in on how pretty you were, I whispered to any and everyone, "Did you know—I mean, I have seen it, don't say I told you—but Pamela Keasey wears a girdle."

A girdle! Something I had seen on my grandmother, who told me it made her look slimmer. I remember watching her jam herself into her girdle—a piece of equipment so rigid it could stand up on its own. A girdle was the perfect ruse.

"It holds in her fat," I said, trying to subtract from your perfectness.

I was rotten. I hated myself for being so bitter and backbiting. But I guess I hated being not as pretty, not as lovely, and not as Pam even more.

I have no excuse, and I cannot blame it on anything except the girdle around my green heart. I would like to tell you that I have corseted my envy, but it would be another lie. When there is a beautiful woman on the movie screen, I turn to my husband and say, "Those aren't real."

I owe you an apology—and possibly a lifetime supply of chocolates or your favorite dessert to make up for my malice.

Some friend,

Ronda

A Letter of Weight

Hello, Vanessa,

A short but heartfelt apology for asking so many questions when our fifth-grade class went on that field trip to the Physics Department at Arizona State University. There in the center of the foyer was, as I recall, a ten-story-tall pendulum. I had never seen anything like it. The professor leading our field trip said that this golden orb, moving back and forth, proves the earth is spinning.

I never was very interested in science, or space, or that kind of stuff, but this was so impressive. I asked a question, then another, and then another; I couldn't stop. I could see me in a white lab coat with black-rimmed glasses carrying a clipboard as I checked on all my experiments. I knew I had found my destiny. Abruptly my dream of being a scientist was interrupted by you yelling, "Ronda, give other people a chance to talk." You looked right at me, clearly disgusted by my gusto.

It was like a light-bulb flash for me—oh, right, other people exist!

My curiosity had clearly swung too far, like, well, a pendulum. In my defense, I was just trying to cover all the angles . . . like a pendulum.

Vanessa, you provided a pivotal moment in my life. You helped me become more aware of my surroundings and the fact that not everyone shares my boundless enthusiasm or loud voice. I instantly realized that I needed to let others get a word in edgewise. This has served me well in all areas of my life, whether friend, leader, teacher, parent, and sometime scientist. All thanks to you.

And I never became a physicist or astronomer, either, although I might have if I had asked a couple more questions. I'll never know . . . all thanks to you.

Yours with no questions asked,

Ronda

A Letter of Exposure

Dear Carolyn King,

We were in the eighth grade together. There is always an outcast in school, always someone who is a target for ridicule and scorn, and—tag!—you were it. I don't know if it was because of your gangly body, your unkempt hair, or your slight accent of some kind; there was no one reason. I suppose it's the subterranean self-loathing of every eighth grader that makes us scour the playground for someone who will bear the brunt of our own miserableness.

You took that brunt and turned it into a cottage industry of sorts by lifting your shirt for boys at twenty-five cents a hoist. I remember seeing this happen in the baseball dugout at recess. I felt the heat of embarrassment, my mouth watered like when I know I am going to vomit, and a sickness that I now know is the burn of injustice took hold of me.

I didn't really know you, Carolyn, but I felt you. It doesn't take long to make a kid feel like a zero, and I can only imagine that exposing yourself is no big deal if you feel like nothing already. And we did that, made fun of you enough that we subtracted and subtracted until showing your chest was all you felt you had to offer.

I marched back to Mr. Fredrick's classroom wiping away tears, determined to tell him what was happening so someone could save you. I rushed into the classroom and approached our teacher. I was clearly and visibly upset, and as I started to tell him what was going on, he looked me right in the eyes and said, "Go sit down."

He said, "Go sit down." Carolyn, he didn't want to hear it, deal with it, or do anything about it. Then he added, as I stood there crying and confused, "It's not your problem."

I walked back to my seat in the front of the room, and when you came in, you walked to yours at the back of the room. I was a kid who was always in the front; you were always in the back. I distinctly remember thinking what always being in the back, being last picked for teams, hoping for a friend or a teacher who cares must feel like. Or how that affects who you become.

I now know, of course, those first eighteen years haunt, hinder, or help you throughout the rest of your life.

I wish I had been able to break up the boys in the dugout, stop the little strip show, and do a movie speech to inspire everyone involved to strive for a home run as a human being, to be a champion on the field of life, to put their balls away (pun on purpose), and use their hearts and minds once in a while. But I could not, did not.

Eighth grade staggered on, high school loomed, I moved to another state, and I witnessed other kids who were left out, laughed at, bullied, or belittled. Carolyn, you opened more than your shirt; you opened my eyes. I have tried throughout my life to fight injustice, cruelty, or malice.

Your pain fueled my path to leadership, whether as a cheerleader, a teacher, or a mother. Your name is on every person I mentor, coach, or care about.

I have no clue where you are or how your life turned out. How I wish you were musician Carole King . . . that would teach 'em!

The people who have faced the darkest hours, the toughest moments, or the worst childhoods are often the most successful and famous. I am hoping your story is one of triumph.

I wanted you to know: I carry you in my life endeavors, and better late than never to tell you . . .

"You've got a friend,"

RONDA

A Letter of Craving

Dear Daddy Bob,

If love could be measured in chocolate malts, I'd be the richest kid on earth. If it were counted in quarters, I'd have a small fortune—minus a few for each time I said, "Huh?" instead of "Pardon me?" (Lesson learned. Mostly.) But if love is simply the way someone's face lights up when they see you, then I won the grandfather lottery.

Spending summers at your house was the highlight of my childhood. And looking back as an adult, I can honestly say—you were the highlight of my life. It's funny how growing older sharpens the view of what truly matters. What matters most. I never told you what you meant to me, never had the words beyond love to express it as more than a noun. I can only pray that I earned and returned your love as a verb—through my laughter, my hugs, my songs, my homemade cards, and the unfiltered joy I felt in your presence.

Home, you taught me, is more than a place. A vital lesson, since my dad, your son, moved our family over twenty times between the years I was in first grade and high school. In that whirlwind, I was always trying—trying to please, trying to get along, trying to find steadiness in the chaos of parents who married at seventeen. I imagine you and Meme weren't thrilled about that choice, but Mom told me that when I was born, all was forgiven—and that you were smitten. Lucky me.

So many firsts with you: my first trip to the dentist, my first beauty parlor haircut, my first fancy dinner out, my first etiquette lessons, in addition to countless reminders of proper English. But most importantly, you were the first man to look at me with unwavering love, acceptance, and joy. I liked that feeling. I needed that feeling. I liked the reflection of me in your eyes—it made me like me. A skinny, talkative kid looking for approval, and in you, I found it. Your love came in so many ways, from warm hugs to quiet lessons to custom-made nightly chocolate milkshakes or malts. (I was always ten pounds heavier by the end of my summers with you!)

I still laugh when I think about the summer you cut my toenails. Meme took a picture of us, and I remember squirming and pretending it hurt, giggling while you held my foot steady. "Your toenails look like owl claws!" you said, shaking your head.

Or the Saturday I walked into the kitchen to find a line of ten quarters on the table.

"You can have all these quarters at the end of the day," you told me.

"Wow!" I jumped and clapped.

"Unless you say, 'Huh?' when we ask you something."

"Huh?" I blurted and watched in horror as you slid a quarter away.

"You can say, 'Pardon?' or 'Excuse me?' or 'Come again?' or 'Sorry, what did you say?' But not 'Huh?'"

I lost one more quarter that day—but I gained so much more. To this day, I never say, "Huh?"

If I could pick the top five moments in my life for a do-over, one of them—if not the first—would be the Christmas you came to visit after Meme died. I was home from college and had a date. Mom said, "Daddy Bob is here to visit. You stay home tonight." You quickly reassured me: "It's OK—go on your date. I'll be here when you get home." And I did.

I want that night back.

I want that time with you back.

I want you back.

No kid really understands how tough it is to be human—to be grown up, to be someone's parent, to be someone's grandparent. Ignorance is one of the blessings of childhood. Ah, but reminiscence, reflection, rewinding the stories and the people who made you, who mentored you, who mattered to you—that is the province of adulthood. And it is both a gift and a reckoning, a bittersweet privilege of time.

Daddy Bob, you are with me every day. In the way I listen. In the way I lift others up. In the way I try to make people feel the way you made me feel—loved, seen, and enough. Your laughter echoes in mine, your kindness shapes my hands, and your quiet strength steadies my heart. The woman I became carries the lessons you left me, not just in memory but in action, in love, and in the life I build. Your legacy isn't just something I remember—it's something I live.

I wish I had told you all of this. But I believe you felt it. In every hug. In every letter I sent when I wasn't with you. In every time I squealed, "Daddy Bob!" the moment I saw you.

I miss you.

Forever your granddaughter.

Ronda

A Letter of Fault

Dear Miss Disotell,

You were my cheerleading adviser for three years—a stretch of time during which I cheered, pledged, pom-pommed, belted out the "Star-Spangled Banner," and shouted, "Go, team!" with every ounce of spirit I had across fields and courts all over Washington State. I wasn't just *on* the squad—I lived and breathed cheerleading. It mattered to me. A lot.

Looking back, it's wild to think we had to cut our hair to chin length just to make the squad. We never questioned that rule—we just did what we were told, like good little girls of that era, ponytails clipped, smiles fixed. I didn't have an anarchist spirit back then, but what I lacked in rebellion, I made up for in exceptional energy and relentless can-do-ism. I held summer practices at my house, choreographed routines (including the one that won us a state championship at cheer camp), and showed up—heart first—every single time.

Yet . . . you seemed hell-bent on giving me demerits.

Forget a yarn flower in my hair? *Demerit.*

A scuff on my saddle shoe? *Demerit.*

Late to practice by thirty seconds? *DEMERIT.*

I racked them up faster than our basketball team racked up fouls. Not once did I get a nod for the things I did right—placing yarn flowers perfectly, leading with enthusiasm, choreographing our routines. Nope. Just your unwavering focus through what felt like demerit-tinted goggles. It felt less like guidance and more like you were keeping score—*as if demerits were trophies, and the more you collected, the better you felt about winning some invisible game.* And I've often wondered: *Why?*

Maybe you were the kind of person who found comfort in control, someone who believed rules were the scaffolding that kept everything from collapsing. Maybe perfection felt like the only way to manage your own uncertainties, so you stacked demerits like defensive stunts—layers of authority designed to keep any vulnerability from showing through. Or maybe, just maybe, you saw my earnestness, my need to be seen and validated, and it irritated you because I was everything you never allowed yourself to be: eager, vulnerable, hungry to be enough.

And what kind of kid cared so much about getting demerits? *Me.*

A kid wired to believe that being "good" equaled being worthy.

A kid who craved gold stars, approval, and the reassurance that I mattered.

A kid who thought that if I just worked harder, jumped higher, smiled wider, maybe—just *maybe*—you'd see me not as a checklist of flaws but as someone who was really trying.

Here's the thing, though: *You didn't break me.*

Sure, I cried into my pom-poms more than once.

Sure, I questioned if I was "enough."

But what you unintentionally taught me was resilience—and maybe, just maybe, the first spark of rebellion. You showed me what leadership shouldn't look like. You taught me that authority without kindness is just control in a shinier outfit.

I'm writing this not out of bitterness (well, maybe with a dash of petty reflection—demerits for scuffed shoes? Really?), but because you were in a position to shape how we saw ourselves. You could've built us up. Instead, for me, it often felt like you were chipping away. I hope—if you're still working with young people—you've learned to inspire rather than intimidate. To see past the scuffed shoes and late arrivals and to recognize heart, effort, and pluck.

Because here's the truth, Miss Disotell: With just a little empathy, a little curiosity about the kid behind the pom-poms, you might have seen the merit in a girl desperate to belong, to shine, to feel worthy in a world that kept shifting beneath her saddle-shoed feet.

Still cheering. Still leading. Still holding my pom-poms high,

RONDA

A Letter of Aloha

Aloha, Donn,

Do you remember giving me the Bob Dylan album *Blood on the Tracks*? I knew, even then, that you were trying to evolve my music tastes, which ran the narrow gamut from Herman's Hermits to Carole King.

You were one of those hippies I had been warned would be plentiful on the Western Washington campus. I was a high school cheerleader with pigtails, wearing pastel-colored turtlenecks and Hush Puppies shoes. How did the same major appeal to both of us? More surprisingly, how did you pull me into Bob Dylan, LSD, and picnics on an Indian reservation? Clearly, it was a "Simple Twist of Fate" . . . see, I did listen to the album.

Allow me the following LPs (letter paragraphs) to explain why it and you mattered to me. I will follow the playlist and poetry of each song on the album. With sincere apologies to Mr. Dylan.

"Tangled Up in Blue"

Early one morning the sun was shining,
I was heading to the classroom
Wond'rin' what I would learn
If it'd be bust or bloom
My folks, they said my life without a degree
Sure was gonna be rough
They never did get to go to school
Daddy's education wasn't big enough
And I was standin' in the hallway
In pink-and-white saddle shoes
Heading out for a broadcast major
That's when I first saw you and got
Tangled up in blue

"You're a Big Girl Now"

Our conversation was short and sweet
Your hair was long, your smile
Swept me off my feet
I felt myself change
I amused you somehow
I'm a big girl now

"Idiot Wind"

The teacher had it in for me
Microphone parts? I had to guess
You came to my rescue that day
And got me outta that mess
We walked after class that day
Took time to know each other
We had so much to say
Idiot Wind
Our profs and parents both
Idiot Wind
To have each other's back
We both took a solemn oath

"You're Gonna Make Me Lonesome When You Go"

LSD came through my door
Brought by someone I didn't know before
Sprinkled on a strawberry, I was gonna take a bite
You flew across the room and gave me a fright
You protected me from acid, we took a walk out in the snow
You're gonna make me lonesome when you go.

Flowers on Lummi Island in spring blooming crazy
Bellingham Bay waves small and lazy
College won't last forever, our enemy is time
I find you in the sunshine, I share you through a rhyme

You gift me with your photos, I paint gulls and sea
We talk of keeping touch, but it wasn't meant to be
You're gonna have to leave me, this I know
You're gonna make me lonesome when you go

"Meet Me in the Morning"

Meet me in the morning
We'll drive to Seattle, meet your folks
I'll see where you came from
Meet me in the morning
Donn, we could be on Lake Washington
By the time the sun is on the run
Your dad is big and brawny
Totally different than you
Your dad is rich, you're scrawny
There are issues here, it's true
I like you better, he loves him, I see
And you and I share this malady

"If You See Her, Say Hello"

If you see me, say hello
Someday you might be near
Graduation came late in spring
You'll be far from here

It's OK, we knew this time would come
I somehow know you'll be all right
You might think you'll be forgotten
In my heart you'll be in sight

And though our separation
It pierced me to the heart
You still live inside of me
We've never been apart

"Shelter from the Storm"

'Twas in another lifetime, homework, books, and such
Did it really help us, maybe not so much
I came in from the suburbs, you a creature not my norm
Come in, I said
I'll give ya shelter from the storm

We never passed that way again, we moved to other roads
Never heard your voice again, not another word
You sailed the ocean, I stayed on land, on that rest assured
In a world of other lives, other friends in other form
Come back, I said
I'll give ya shelter from the storm

"Buckets of Rain"

Buckets of rain
Buckets of years
Got all them buckets and they're filled with tears
Wishing for old days when we took a stand
A special friend
Who took me by the hand
Buckets of rain
Long ago far away
Living each year in skies of gray
College and growing up some
Meeting you became where I was from

I love the memory,
I loved your style
Liked the way you made me smile
We did what we did, and we did it well
Hope this letter finds you happy and well.

So, Donn, "aloha" means hello and goodbye. Staying in touch is impossible, I understand, because touch goes away. All I have are words, and a borrowed playlist, to finally share that our college friendship, your place in my life, was an uncommon composition.

Just like a woman, but I break just like a little girl,
Ronda

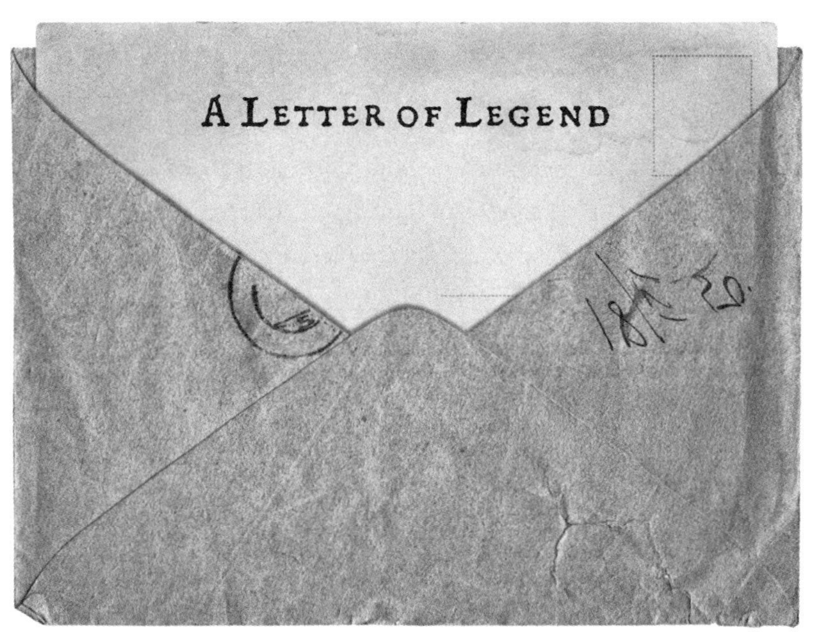
A Letter of Legend

Dear friend, mentor, superstar, and lifelong role model,

Walking into your new fitness studio on Van Nuys Boulevard was a moment that changed everything for me. Because of that fateful day, I have had labrum tears, meniscus issues, a broken wrist, dancer's hip, a wired toe, and more—and I couldn't be more grateful.

I was visiting my parents, and my dad had furnished a car for the movie you were shooting, *The China Syndrome*. He was smitten, I could tell, and he told me you had just started this fitness business, and he suggested I go check it out. This was an improvement over his usual suggestion that I go play on the freeway, so I obliged.

The next morning, I walked into your studio, and *you* were teaching! I couldn't believe it. You welcomed me with a firm handshake and open smile and introduced yourself simply as "Jane." You struck me not as someone famous but someone special. Kind, open, generous. That first impression has held fast throughout your life and mine. You were so down-to-earth and real—qualities the public might not expect, but qualities that have made you my lifelong inspiration. Let's face it: You don't have to be real, or honest, or even nice—your talent and pedigree and star power could absolve you from dealing with earthlings.

That morning in your class, I pushed myself harder physically than ever before. I kicked higher, smiled wider, laughed more freely, and even sang out loud. I threw my big hair around with confidence, smiled though my sweat, whooped a few times all in an effort to impress you—and I did! You asked me if I would be interested in teaching, and before you could finish the offer, I yelped, "Yes!"

I had always wanted dance lessons; actually, always wanted to be famous . . . but famous for helping others and inspiring people to be better than they thought they could be. I was neither, but you were, are, both of those and more. From that day on, you became my role model and beacon for what is possible if you work hard enough, believe deeply enough, and speak up with heart and hope.

I had never known a woman to speak out, to protest wrongdoings, to take the slings and arrows of having an opinion, to risk it all for what she felt was right . . . until you. I know I am not alone when I say that your example made me a stronger, more self-respecting, and fitter person.

I have taught workouts in the back room of a beauty parlor, on the runway of a local airport, in malls across the country, and more. I currently teach boot camp and barre, and I am the creator of a fitness class that is sent globally online to special-needs students. I use these fitness classes as a vehicle to remind people of their divinity, their potential, their worth, and the just plain wonder of being alive and getting their turn on the planet. Everything I do, contribute, or exemplify has your name on it.

Speaking of your name, at one point my parents thought I was overdoing the exercise thing and mentioned they thought I was spending too much time doing workouts. I laughed it off and said, "I want to look as good as Jane Fonda when I am her age."

My dad quickly replied, "You don't look that good now."

That's another story.

Anyway, you fight for what you believe, stand up for what you think is right, and welcome criticism for unpopular opinions. When I was growing up, there was only Mary Tyler Moore and Marlo Thomas, and they were cute and funny and forging new paths, but they were characters. You are real. You have shared real pain, real disappointment, and real truth all along your development as a woman and as a person. A real person. The real deal. My heroine.

Thank you.

This entire book could, and maybe should, be dedicated to you. I didn't have parents who were particularly interested in me, no exemplary teachers other than in first grade, and no mentor until I met you. To paraphrase Ralph Waldo Emerson, "To know one life has been bettered because you have lived, this is success." I hope this trumps or at least ties the Oscars and Emmys on your shelves!

Thank you, Jane, for showing me real success, for believing in me at first sight, and for sharing your talents, time, and truth with me . . . and the rest of the world.

If we were sisters, I'd be Ronda Fonda,

RONDA

A Letter of Triumph

Hey, Multiple Sclerosis,

I've heard from you. I think it's finally time you hear from me.

You arrived suddenly—silent, unwelcome, and with no intention of leaving. I was in graduate school, standing at the edge of a life I had worked so hard to build, when you slipped in through the back door of my nervous system and tried to rewrite my story.

You came bearing uncertainty. You came with whispered threats—of canes, of wheelchairs, of limitation. A future lived in slow motion. But I had other plans. Big ones. Loud ones. Plans that involved movement, purpose, sweat, laughter, and a refusal to play victim.

I made you my sparring partner, not my sentence. I chose to live not in spite of you, but *beyond* you. You have never been the headline of my life, only the fine print—one paragraph in a long, high-impact story I continue to write every single day.

You may reside in my brain and spine, but you do not own me. I picture you often—not as a monster, not even as a disease—but as a pattern of snowflakes, those tiny white spots on my MRI. I see them as fleeting and fragile, melting each night in my mind's eye. I will not feed you with fear. You do not grow stronger in the dark. You shrink in my light.

You do not define me.

You refine me.

I've stayed fit. Taught others to move with joy and strength. I've refused to make you the center of my story. And perhaps that's why you've remained, for the most part, quiet. I haven't had to take medication. I haven't given up adventure. I haven't shrunk my life to fit your demands.

If anything, you've made me better. More patient. More forgiving. More curious about the unseen burdens others carry. You slowed me down just enough to notice more, to feel more, to lead with more compassion. You taught me that adversity can be an invitation—an opening—to live more intentionally.

And you've taught me resilience—because nothing builds character like being stalked by a chronic condition with boundary issues.

You may have pressed "Pause" on parts of my nervous system. But I hit "Play" on everything else.

I know you're not done. I know you may try again. But I am not afraid of you. You are part of my story, but you are not my identity. I am still writing the rest—on my feet, with purpose, and in motion. And if you try to rise again, know this: I am ready. With grace as my armor and grit as my sword, I will meet you—stronger, wiser, and utterly unwilling to back down.

I have MS.

But MS does not have me.

And frankly, you picked the wrong girl.

Yours, never,

Ronda

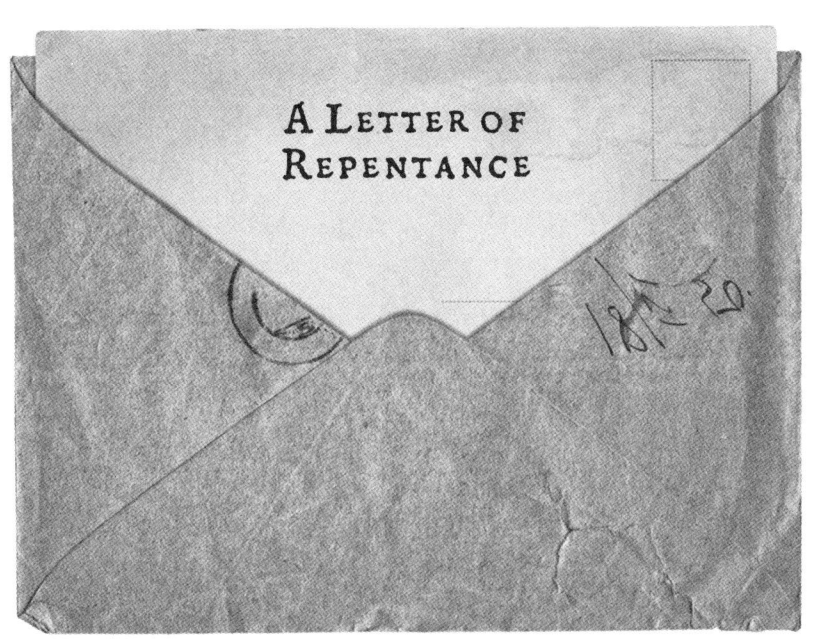
A Letter of
Repentance

Dear Scott,

Yesterday I walked into the house of a young friend who had invited me on her podcast. I was expecting and prepared for microphones, computers, and lots of extension cords.

Instead, on the floor lay scattered toys, a lone tiny sock (Why is it always just one sock?), broken crayons, deflated balloons, and a stray ribbon of crepe paper—fluttering like a forgotten whisper from some past birthday.

I was totally caught off guard by the sight, the baby powder smells, being amid the controlled chaos, and it pierced right into the heart of the young mother I once was—the one who had cradled small hands and soothed midnight fears—and slammed me with the unrelenting truth of the past I cannot change, which brought my thoughts to you and what I owe you.

How do I apologize to you? Let me count the ways.

The tableau I took in yesterday was oh-so-reminiscent of our house when we were married, with two baby boys and wearing the constant look of young parents, in their moment of cosmic realization—the one where they grasp that *everything* their child becomes depends on *them*—a look like a deer in headlights . . . if the deer were also holding a mortgage, running on two hours of sleep, and suddenly remembering they never learned how to fold a fitted sheet properly.

I know you remember the mix of awe, terror, and the dawning awareness that our own parents were probably winging it too. We had a flicker of confidence—"We got this!"—immediately followed by panic—"Do we got this?"—and then resignation—"Well, guess we're making it up as we go."

Somewhere between the first diaper disaster and the first unsolicited parenting advice from a stranger at the grocery store, we realized: *Oh no, we are the grown-ups now.*

But we weren't grown-ups, were we? We were just two kids trying to figure out love, life, and ourselves. And being college sweethearts isn't much of a training ground for being married or being parents.

And then there were the handicaps—one set of parents married at seventeen, the other lost to alcohol. We weren't just navigating love; we were dodging the ruin of what came before us. Maybe we never stood a chance.

Looking back now, with all the years and distance between us, I see so clearly what I couldn't back then—I didn't know myself well enough to know what love truly required. I was young, unformed, and chasing a version of happiness that was more about escaping than building. I made choices that served me, that gave me room to grow, but in doing so, I severed something that wasn't mine alone to break. I was immature, selfish in ways I didn't recognize at the time, and blind to the weight of the promises I made before I understood what keeping them really meant. And for the pain that caused—for the hurt that lived beyond us—I am deeply apologetic.

I know my path took me away, and in doing so, it took the boys away too. That choice changed all of us in ways I can't fully measure, and I'm not writing to justify or undo any of it—just to say that I carry an awareness of what that must have been like for you.

Becoming a single mother was an instant reckoning—a crash course in responsibility, sacrifice, and the kind of strength I didn't know I had. There was no room for immaturity, no space for self-indulgence. Every decision suddenly carried weight, every dollar had to stretch, and every dream had to make room for survival. I learned, quickly and sometimes painfully, what it meant to build a life that wasn't just about me anymore. And in that fire, I became someone stronger, wiser—someone I can be proud of. But I also know that my growth came at a cost. That in finding my own way, I left wreckage behind. The hurt I caused you, the pain our sons carried—those are things I can't undo. And while I wouldn't trade the lessons I've learned, I regret, deeply, the price others, especially you, had to pay for them.

I am sad for the birthdays we didn't celebrate, the crepe paper we never hung, the socks we didn't search for together, the milestones I stole from you, and the role of Dad I denied you.

I need a better, bigger, more encompassing word; *sorry* is too small, too limited, too overused to convey what I am trying to say . . . maybe a word that truly holds the depth of regret, sorrow, apology, and the weight of irreversible choices. The remorse I have and the ordeal I put you through . . . *remordeal.* I am remordeal for leaving, for taking, for breaking what we had.

Yet despite everything, we found our way through. Time carried us forward, reshaping our lives in ways we never could have imagined back when we were just two kids fumbling through love and parenthood. The loss was real, and so was the pain—but so, too, was the strength that grew from it. You built a life. I built one, too, and somehow, through all the remains and all the years, our sons found their own ways as well.

I don't know if life ever truly gives us a way to balance the scales, to make things right in the way we wish we could. But if nothing else, I hope you know that I see you, that I respect the man, father, and now friend you are, and that I carry gratitude alongside my remordeal. For what we had, for what we lost, and for what we somehow still share in the two incredible people we brought into this world.

Remordeally,

Ronda

A Letter of Trajectory

Mr. Mason,

No, no matter what Paul Simon says, I can't just call you Al.

I know it's your name, but I just can't . . . even after all this time, and I am now older than you were when we met. You are and will remain Mr. Mason. My role model, father figure, mentor, and, as you sign your letters to me, my humble servant from afar.

Like it was yesterday, I remember standing in the snowy field outside the Best Western in Shippensburg, waiting for a ride to my interview to teach at the university. I was shivering, not from the cold, but from nerves.

In the distance I saw a horse and carriage coming my way. I thought, "Wow! It's like Central Park; they are taking me to campus in a carriage!" As the carriage clip-clopped by me, the driver—dressed in black clothes and hat with a long beard—gave the horse a bit of whip and stared sternly at me. I was not in California anymore.

"Amish," you said when you picked me up. Everything about that day was new. Except you. I felt right at home in this foreign place; you were an old friend I just met. I loved you instantly and felt protected and promoted with each introduction and during each interview.

We often laugh about my creative résumé, the one within a 45-record sleeve with my picture on one side and *RONDA'S RECORD* on the flip side. It was the reason you called me for the job, intrigued by who would send a résumé like that. "*But*," you said, "I am not sure our dean can handle this, so do you have a 'regular' résumé we can give him?"

Again, you were my champion, explaining to the dean why I was a stellar candidate and why I would be a lauded addition to the faculty. He already had a copy of my *RONDA'S RECORD* résumé and looked up as you handed him the "regular" résumé, saying, "You didn't think I could handle this one, did you, Mr. Mason?" We both froze, looked at one another, and then joined the dean in laughing. I got the job.

You taught me to teach. You gave me encouragement for many of my "creative" approaches to engaging students. Do you remember me staging a fake news event for the journalism students that involved kidnapping? Masked students came into my classroom and forced me out of the building and into a getaway car. The problem was I forgot to tell campus police, who arrived with sirens and flashing lights and guns. Made for quite the front-page story, but not the one I had intended!

Thank you for giving me your lake cabin to live in. My young sons were arriving, and I had not found a house. This would be the first place we would live together without their dad, as the divorce was imminent. The tears, the sadness, the ache of it all was ameliorated by canoeing, having cookouts, and telling stories at night around the fireplace. As a father of five, you instinctively knew what my boys needed and took them birding, taught them photography, and gave us all a soft place to land, under your wing.

I am reminded of the old movie *To Sir, with Love*. By the end of their time together, the students realize how much they have grown, what critical lessons Sir has imparted, and how much love he shared with them. Not for reward or award, but because it was simply, yet powerfully, who he was . . . a conduit of love, and hope, and promise.

Forty years have passed since we met. The Amish still pull their carriages by horse down King Street; I am still standing in front of university students hoping to instruct and inspire. Each lecture, assignment, or project has your name on it, your heart in it, and your guidance at the core.

We are both approaching our final, final exam, but if John Adams is right (and he always is), our profession is the closest to immortality. We may never know how or who or why, but there will be moments for decades, or perhaps eternity, that our lessons are shared, our teaching recalled, and even our names mentioned.

I have had the most animated and lively professional life, and it started when you picked me up on that snowy day in Shippensburg. You gave me my big chance; you provided the path and paved my way. I have really treasured the experience of teaching and have developed a deep reverence for the calling.

One that almost equals the love and reverence I have for you, Mr. Mason. It is beyond measure and beyond the name Al.

With all my heart, all I have become, and all that I will leave behind,
Ronda

A Letter of
Enchantment

Abracadabra, David Copperfield!

When I first saw your magic show, I already had a doctorate in education, had been instructed by at least one hundred different teachers, was a university professor, and in one hour of wizardry, you became the best educator I had ever seen. Or may ever see.

Sure, there were dancing-tissue tricks, the old sleight-of-hand stuff, and each trick more astonishing than the last. But as I watched, it occurred to me that just as a magician makes a trick look seamless, a great teacher should make learning feel natural and engaging. And even though there's a lot of preparation and practice behind the scenes, as they say, "Never let them see you sweat."

The best magicians make people believe in the impossible. The best teachers make students believe in their own impossibilities. A great magic trick stays with you forever. A great lesson—or a great teacher—can change a student's life forever.

It wasn't just the illusions that captivated me—it was the way you wove stories, emotion, and meaning into each trick. You created moments that left the audience astounded and deeply moved. Watching you, I realized that my role as a teacher wasn't just to present information but to create an experience—one that made learning feel just as wondrous as watching you walk through the Great Wall of China or make the Statue of Liberty disappear.

You shared the story of being a little boy and seeing your first snow. Presto! A little boy appeared next to you, conjured from nowhere. There you both stood as you continued telling the story of your boyhood home, memories of your parents, and the wonder of the world when you were young and everything was fresh, well, as fallen snow. And the music rose, the lights dimmed, and snow began to fall in Gammage Hall at Arizona State University. A hush fell on the crowd, many audience members were crying, and we were all children again, faces turned up, eyes closed, feeling the snow, remembering home, and leaning into who we had once been. Children in the room were catching flakes, delighted by the glistening beauty, and I could hear them whispering,

"Awesome." Awe, Mr. Copperfield, so hard to come by in a world subjugated by the rectangular gloom-and-doom machine we hold in our hand. What sorcery!

Your magic taught me that every lesson should have a sense of mystery, a buildup to discovery, and a moment of revelation. Like a magician, a teacher must carefully craft an illusion—making the difficult seem effortless, guiding students to their own "aha" moments, and ensuring that the impact lasts long after the class ends.

I started to think about my lessons the way you think about your performances. How could I engage my students so fully that they forgot they were even learning? How could I create moments of wonder that would stay with them long after they left my classroom? Your illusions helped me see that teaching isn't just about content—it's about crafting an experience that students will never forget.

Almost immediately I indulged in professorial prestidigitation, a ta-da approach. I employed costumes, skits, music; I told stories to make my points; I created teach-ins; took speech students out of the classroom to assisted living centers to present; turned a four-hundred-student class into a talk show with a live band and guests; used students' talents to sing, dance, write poetry, or use art to tell their stories, all aimed at the finale: learning that lasts. My students volunteered at germane organizations, wrote editorials for public radio, created feature films, and built libraries for Head Start and schools in Africa. I created lessons that were, if I do say so myself . . . magic.

Many awards came my way, including the National Education Association Art of Teaching Award, but the real win was the alchemy of the students, the hocus-pocus of purpose in their studies.

Your artistry shaped the way I teach and, in turn, has shaped the way thousands of my students learn. And that is its own kind of magic. Bravo.

Giving you a permanent standing ovation,

Ronda

A Letter of Remorse

Marcia,

I knew you all my life. We shared a room until I was sixteen, as well as secrets, stories, and back scratches. In fact, I still owe you one thousand from the night I was ten and you were eight and I told you I would repay one thousand back scratches . . . I would scratch yours if you scratched mine. And you did. And I didn't. The failure to return the favor became a joke to me, an irk for you. This was the flavor of our relationship. You were kind, generous, and believing. Me, bossy and often sneaky and selfish.

I chalk it up to being all part of growing up. Learning to be a better person, learning to be true to your word, learning to be someone better, someone good, someone more. Well, at least part of my growing up, it seems, more than yours. You didn't need those lessons.

You were unfailingly kind as a child, generous, and full of curiosity and fun. You had faith in me, our parents, our brother. To your everlasting detriment, you even had faith in your faithless husband and the father of your children. You looked up to all of us, and we let you down more often than not.

Did you know you were beautiful? You had a flair, which I lacked, of looking good in everything and walking into a room with a quiet grace and a simple elegance. You also had a flat stomach. I was so jealous. Plus, you were taller than me, true, but that is not why I looked up to you. I secretly wished to be seen as poised and calm as you seemed to be. One day while I was visiting Daddy's office, a coworker walked in and said, "Ron, you didn't tell me you had a beautiful daughter." Without missing a beat, our father said, "This is the smart one; the beautiful one is at home."

Beauty is as beauty does. Marcia, you were so thoughtful. Angsting for hours over what gifts to give people, shopping for days or weeks to find just the right present or spending hours to make it. The sunflower mosaic keepsake box you made me with the words "I Love You" written inside is an enduring treasure that holds a place of honor in my living room. I wish you knew that.

My favorite memories are of you and me baking brownies and watching

Fred Astaire movies. Watching *White Christmas,* singing "Sisters"—me Rosemary Clooney and you Mitzi Gaynor (her stomach was flat). Dressing as geishas to cook stir-fry dinner for our parents. Decorating the Christmas trees of our childhood. I know we loved each other in the unspoken and testy way sisters do.

And then we left each other right when we needed each other most. I left for different states and spouses; you left for sustenance and solace in a bottle. Your grace and fragility, your belief in love, and hope, and promises shattered like a whiskey glass, along with your self-control and self-esteem.

I made attempts to help, but they were feeble, and I was judgmental. My apology is late and futile. None of your sons call me Aunt; well, none of your sons call me at all. I deserve their distance. But you were right when you told me, "They are all so good and happy and successful, I must have done something right."

Marcia, you did so many things right, and the world often could not match your big, big heart. I remember the time you wanted to see what fun the neighbor kids were having yelling and laughing as they played in their yard. You climbed the fence to say hello, and the boy next door hit you in the face with a bamboo pole, leaving a scar on your face the rest of your life.

Life kept smacking you, and we, me, failed to stitch you back together in a healing and healthy way. I hope you somehow know how much you have been loved, how the loss of your soul leaves an irreplaceable space in the world, and how deeply I hope you have found peace. If we meet again, I promise to repay the thousand back scratches you have been owed for so long.

Your sister,

Ronda

A Letter of Romance

Dear Miles,

You were a priest, I was married, but that didn't stop me from falling in love.

Sitting next to each other on the flight to Kyoto, we talked, we laughed, we sipped white wine and ate crackers and cheese. It is only now, writing that sentence, I realize you performed a high-altitude Communion.

We were both set to speak at the same event, stay at the same hotel. My husband would arrive on a later flight. We made a date to reconnect that night at the hotel bar before said husband arrived.

Landing in Japan alone was no longer a foreign or daunting experience for me; it was an affair of the heart.

I unpacked, showered, and readied for our date while rehearsing what I would tell my husband about you, about us.

The bar was dimly lit, smoky, and cinematic. You ordered Chablis, and I celebrated our reunion with champagne. I listened to you explain priesthood and giggled at your stories and jokes, all the while wondering if you, like me, had read *The Thorn Birds*. Maybe you saw the movie?

You walked me back to my room, gave me an innocent and gentlemanly kiss on the cheek, asked me to call you Mimi, and said good night. I could see signs of the song-and-dance man you had been as a young man as you skipped and kick-ball-chained back to the elevator that would take you to your room and away from me. Parting was such sweet sorrow, Mimi.

My husband's knock at the door woke me from a jet-lagged but heart-lifted sleep. I ran to the door without my robe, threw open the door with naked abandon, literally, and admitted I was in love with another man . . . and I couldn't wait for him to meet you. Needless to say, sleeping was not the priority that night, but I promised my husband he would understand and approve once he met you.

The next morning, I convinced him to attend your presentation with me, to see for himself the how and why of our romance. After watching you masterfully engage, entertain, and educate the attendees . . . not surprisingly he fell in love with you too.

In fact, the entire room swooned. All attendees were besotted, and we couldn't walk anywhere the rest of the day with you without being stopped multiple times by people needing a hug, asking you to speak with them about their children, wanting advice, or taking a piece of your glow during each encounter.

You, Father Miles, are a love magnet. At an age when most mere mortals are taking naps and using canes, you possessed the most energy, widest smile, and quickest wit of anyone at the Young Presidents' Organization (YPO).

No one thought that you might be tired or that you might need a hug or a hand. You live on a one-way, Miles O'Brien Riley, street. It is a heavily trafficked road traveled by thousands of those you have performed catechism for, given solace to, helped, or healed in hundreds of ways at all hours, on any day or night. Your Christlike example almost turned this Methodist into a Catholic.

By the way, whom do I talk to about making sainthood official? Perhaps a letter to the pope on your behalf . . . I won't say a word about our kiss.

I love you still, Mimi. Just those few precious and memorable days with you in a land far, far away gave me new insights into selfless love, patient compassion, and the power of a bawdy joke told perfectly . . . "Two pickets to Tittsburgh, please."

You remain my favorite story to tell, my best-loved chance encounter, and my exemplar of an extraordinary human being.

Ronda

PS: My husband says hello.

A Letter of Gratitude

Dear Unknown Member of the Olmecs,

I would first like to extend my deepest gratitude and admiration for your courage. It takes a bold and perhaps slightly unhinged soul to spot a lumpy, odd-shaped pod dangling from a tree and think, "Ah, yes. I shall crack this open and see what's inside!"

I can only imagine the moment of discovery. There you stood, in the thick, humid air of the jungle, eyes gleaming with curiosity. With an eager hand, you pried open the mysterious pod, only to find a cluster of seeds, glistening in a rather unappetizing manner. But did that stop you? No, of course not. You forged ahead, a true pioneer of taste, plucking a seed and popping it into your mouth.

And then—what a mistake. The overwhelming bitterness assaulting your unsuspecting tongue. Or whatever you called it. Perhaps you spat it out. Perhaps you cursed the heavens. Perhaps you clutched at your throat, waving wildly at your companions, who were now deeply regretting letting you lead the food discovery expedition. But did you give up? No. No, you did not.

Instead, you must have thought, "Surely, this can be improved!" So through what I can only assume was a combination of sheer persistence and perhaps a desperate need to salvage your dignity, you dried the seeds, ground them, mixed them with water, and—still bitter. Perhaps at this stage, your fellow tribesmen advised you to let it go. "No way," you must have uttered in Olmec. You knew, deep in your soul, that something glorious lurked within this frumpy pod.

You would show them.

Then, in an act of divine inspiration (or sheer desperation), you thought to add sugar. Or sap, or something sweet. A little stirring, a little tasting . . . and behold . . . whatever gods you worshipped smiled down on you and this new concoction you called . . . bitter water.

Well, yes, the name needed work.

But from that first sip of rich, sweet, intoxicating mixture came what was eventually called chocolate. And for this, dear, dear Olmec tribe member, I thank you. I thank you on behalf of every person who has ever unwrapped a bar after a long day, every child with a sticky, chocolate-covered grin, and every soul who has ever been healed by a cup of warm cocoa on a cold night.

You, persistent Olmec, are history's true hero and someone I fervently thank daily.

Forever in your debt (and possibly in possession of too many chocolate bars),

Ronda

A Letter of
Commencement

Dear Dr. Seuss,

I read that your father wanted you to earn a doctorate, but you never did. You just added Dr. to your pen name. Genius! Which you were in imagination and stories that got kids interested in reading, of course, but I wish I had thought of just adding Dr. to my name. It took me twelve years, what I like to call the Dirty Dozen, to earn mine.

When I was slated to give a university commencement address to over ten thousand people, I knew they would introduce me as Dr. Beaman. "No one is going to be impressed by my doctorate; there will be hundreds of Dr. Whatevers there," I thought.

I decided that the first sentence of the speech was going to be, "I am trying to think of doctors you respect and admire to guide me on this important occasion. Perhaps Dr. J, maybe Dr. Phil, or Dr. Dre? And then it hit me, someone everyone in this stadium knows and loves . . . Dr. Seuss!" At which point I donned a red-striped Cat in the Hat hat and delivered a rhyming, whimsical, but meaningful commencement address à la you. In fact, I might have done an "Oh, the Places You Will Go" before you did!

I was the first person in my family to go to college. My parents were in high school when they had me, which dashed my father's dreams of becoming, well, becoming anything. And deep down I believe he held his life letdowns against me. He said so in different ways. When I got my first professorship at a small university in Pennsylvania, we toured the campus together, and he said to me, "Good professors teach at Harvard and Princeton and places like that, right?"

Dr. Seuss, I wish you had seen, or I could have told you, that my speech, inspired by you, garnered a massive eruption of applause and hoorays from that entire stadium (not including my fellow faculty, who stayed seated and grinched), which gave me a five-minute standing ovation. On my way back to my car after the ceremony, parents yelled across the parking lot, "That was the best speech ever!" "You made graduation awesome!" "Thank you, that was amazing." And on and on!

My commencement address made front-page news and was shared for many months with graduates and their families, who all requested their own copies. You would have been delighted, I think, by the homage.

My father did not come to the event, but I had a video of it, and my mother asked if they could see it.

I brought them the DVD, which flickered on with the caption "University Graduation Ceremony Highlights."

"Highlights? If these are the highlights, you will not be on this one, Ronda," my father quipped, looking straight ahead at the screen.

The opening scene showed me sitting with about twenty other professors in full academic regalia. I was sitting on a folding metal chair. I looked tiny, unsure, and very nervous.

"Ladies and gentlemen, honored guests, faculty, students, and family members, we are proud to introduce our speaker today, Dr. Ronda Beaman. She is the top-rated teacher at our university and has been recognized as the President's Teaching Scholar of the Year. She has been named the National Education Association's first Art of Teaching award winner. In addition, she was selected as Outstanding Graduate Student, and her dissertation in education garnered the top prize for scholarly work at Arizona State University, where she graduated with high honors."

I felt sickly self-conscious, and my head began to throb. I tried to poke fun at me before he did and laughed nervously, saying, "Ha ha, great piece of creative writing, huh, Daddy?" I was looking at him, smiling weakly.

He did not respond to or acknowledge my attempt to divert him from the awkward recitation of my résumé as the emcee continued.

"Before entering academe, Dr. Beaman worked in television, hosting a regional show, and then turned her talents to public relations and marketing, eventually owning her own company. She is a published author and travels internationally as a speaker and consultant.

"In her spare time"—at this there is laughter from the audience, but none in front of the TV set—"Dr. Beaman is a fitness trainer and executive coach.

Please join me in welcoming our speaker, Dr. Ronda Beaman."

Hearing my introduction, sitting next to my father and struggling to tamp down all the raw emotion and ignore all the recriminating evidence of our relationship, I wished I could tell him that a more truthful introduction would also state that I slept only four hours a night for decades, that my determination to amount to something cost me a marriage, and that I have fought my way through disfiguring cancer and multiple sclerosis. I wondered if my father would approve of me, or appreciate my journey a little, if he knew about the tough stuff too.

I found I was embarrassed by the litany of "look at me" accomplishments I heard in my introduction. What seemed inspired at the time I was living it sounded insipid listed out loud. My introduction was clearly the introduction of someone who went to great lengths to impress somebody.

And that somebody was sitting next to me.

My father didn't move a muscle and was in the same position as when the video started. I was sitting to his right, so I couldn't see his face or read his mind. But after all these years, and with his voice always in my head, I could guess. The caption bubble would now say, "Those who can, do . . . those who can't, become teachers . . . like Ronda."

"Wait a minute," I told myself. "No one paved the way for me, handed me a silver spoon or even a hand. I had to keep trying, losing, trying again, failing and flailing to be my best. I should be proud . . . of what I have done, of who I have become . . . he should be proud."

I remained proud of myself for at least five more minutes until the video ended with the promised ten-thousand-person standing ovation. I blushed and broke into a discomforting sweat. I began a silent countdown, waiting for him to launch the critique, cutting remark, or joke he would tell to leave me feeling wounded and inconsequential.

"Five . . . four . . . three . . ."

Instead, I beheld something akin to Halley's Comet, the aurora borealis, and rain in the Gobi Desert all in one fell swoop.

I saw one tear drop from his right eye, as he stared at the now blank and buzzing television screen. I watched it drip down his cheek, dropping onto his chest. I was unblinking and mesmerized, like a chemist studying a rare and previously unseen life-form under the microscope, as I studied the parsimonious fluid spreading on my father's cotton shirt. He didn't look at me but at last uttered, "I had no idea."

Dr. Seuss, your father may have wanted you to earn a doctorate, but instead, you gifted the world with wisdom far deeper than any degree could confer. And somehow, through your irreverent rhymes, boundless imagination, and sneaky doses of truth, you became the father figure I most needed—one who believed in possibility, who said I could be more, do more, become more, even when the voices closest to me didn't. My father had no idea, but you had plenty of them.

You lit my path with whimsy, not judgment. With courage, not comparison. And in your honor— from one of my favorite books of yours, *Oh, the Thinks You Can Think*—I've tried to live a life of "funny things that make you think, and thinking things that make you smile." Thank you for showing me that, as you say in *Oh, the Places You'll Go*, "You have brains in your head. You have feet in your shoes. You can steer yourself any direction you choose." Because of you, I chose to rise. I chose to speak. And I chose, finally, to believe that I mattered. So I say, and most people think you said, "Don't cry because it's over; smile because it happened"—and thank you, Dr. Seuss, for happening to me.

With a standing ovation for you,

RONDA

A Letter of Devotion

Dear Student of the EDF 200 School,

We built your school.

Yes, I—along with three hundred education majors at Northern Arizona University—helped build it. And though we may never walk its halls or see your smile as you sit in one of its classrooms, I can tell you with absolute certainty: *It is one of the most meaningful things we have ever done.*

I imagine you each day—tying your shoes, adjusting your uniform, slinging your bag over your shoulder, and walking dusty roads that stretch longer than we can imagine. Roads that are sometimes hard, sometimes dangerous, but ones you travel with determination. I cannot fully understand what you face—the distances, the challenges, the responsibilities at home, the hunger that sometimes growls louder than the lessons. But I see the strength it must take to rise every morning, to choose education when it would be easier not to. *That strength is what inspired us to build your school.*

Did anyone tell you how we did it? How we turned a dream into walls, windows, and open doors for you?

We created a TEACH-IN—a gathering filled with passion, creativity, and a whole lot of heart. My college students—future teachers—came together for twenty-four hours, teaching five-minute lessons under the sky, camping out on campus, raising money not for themselves but for *you*. There were fire-eaters, dancers, jugglers, poets, singers—each of them nervous, hopeful, and full of the belief that what they were doing mattered. And it did. They may not have known your name, but they believed in your future. Every lesson taught, every dollar raised, carried the hope that you would walk through the doors of that school and dream bigger dreams than we ever could.

And now, here you are—*the dream we built, walking, thinking, learning.*

You may not have fire-eaters at your school, but I bet you have something even better—classmates who surprise you with hidden talents, teachers who believe in you, and lessons that plant seeds in your heart. *Education is full of quiet magic.* Sometimes, it's not loud or obvious, but it grows inside you like roots stretching deep into the earth, anchoring you even when the winds of life blow hard.

Imagine the desert where you live. At first glance, it may seem dry and barren, but look closer—life is everywhere. Strong plants with deep roots, surviving and thriving. *That's you.* Every lesson you learn, every question you ask, every time you choose to show up—you're growing invisible roots. And one day, you'll realize you've grown something beautiful: knowledge, confidence, and a future full of possibilities.

I know school isn't always easy. Even in the cool school we built for you. But education is more than just facts—it's the key to doors you haven't even discovered yet. *It's the passport to a life where you choose your own path.* Whether you dream of being a teacher, a doctor, an artist, an engineer, or a leader in your community—school is your first step.

So, dear student, though an ocean separates us, *we are with you.* We are with you as you walk to school, as you sit with your books, and as you wonder about your future. We are with you in your struggles, in your victories, and in the quiet moments when you think no one notices how hard you're trying.

We built your school. Now you build your future. Nourish those seeds. Grow your trees. Dream your dreams.

With love, pride, and belief in you,

Dr. Ronda Beaman

Teacher, Fundraiser, and Tree Grower

A Letter of Magnitude

Dear Student Teacher,

I remember being nineteen and waking up in the middle of the night with cold sweats, thinking, "Wait, you mean I work hard at school, I suffer through statistics, plod through Beckett, graduate, get a job, and no matter what I learn, earn, give, or get, no matter whom I love, where I go, how I contribute, or change the world for the better . . . I still *die*?"

Shakespeare? Dead.

Newton? Gone.

Albert Schweitzer? Goner.

Mother Teresa? So long.

Stephen Hawking? Poof.

Sure, I had lost goldfish, dogs, cats, and even a beloved grandmother . . . but I guess it had never hit me that it, death, would hit *me*.

You've had that reckoning, too, I bet. It's a sucker punch, a cold shower, and a bad breakup all in one fell swoop.

It's *unfair*.

"Whoever told you life was fair?" my father always said when denying me permission or pleasure.

"Yeah, but . . ." was my only available reply.

Turns out "yeah, but" works as well when confronting existential angst as it did when asking to raise my allowance.

"Yeah, but I am a good person." Great, people will come to your funeral.

"Yeah, but I am a wealthy person." OK. You get an expensive funeral.

"Yeah, but I eat well, exercise daily, and don't smoke or drink." Your life may not be longer than anyone else's; it will just seem like it.

What a rude awakening those many years ago, and it still bugs me. It's a lousy deal. But it is the deal.

So what to do? How to live? How to matter? Why matter?

Choices include the following:

Sex, drugs, and rock and roll . . . perfect for college students or Aerosmith.

Religion . . . promising for those who believe in mortal coils and immortal souls, including popes and Scientologists.

Wealth, power, title . . . visit Carnegie schools, Rockefeller museums, or Apple's new headquarters . . . you won't find the guy with his name on the sign anywhere.

Self-sacrifice for family . . . an hour or two after you die, everyone goes to get something to eat—riding in the car you bought for them (maybe Dad), or following a recipe for mac and cheese (perhaps Mother).

Then there is what you are doing . . . teaching.

And done right, teaching is the single element of potential greatness in any position, job, or task.

Teaching is not the same as leading.

Teaching is not the same as being the boss.

Teaching is not the same as parenting.

Teaching is not the same as being an artist.

But teaching can be and should be the utmost asset for meaning and mattering in these and many other jobs, gigs, offices, or efforts.

True teaching doesn't happen only or often in a classroom. Teaching happens when learning, change, and growth happen.

Think of your profession, your job, or your position. All of us, in one way or another, are, by design or default, teachers.

And no matter what you do for a living, being a teacher can give the major part of your day and ultimately your life a touch of immortality.

I declared that night of death-inspired despair, lying in bed in my college dorm, "I will find a way to live, a way to matter. I refuse to be irrelevant; I will not be a waste of skin."

My roommate told me to shut up and go back to sleep.

And from that night on, I have never really done either. For those of us who are really awake, life is amazing, and those of us who teach become eternal.

I have run political campaigns; created advertising that blew up Jack in the Box; hosted television and radio shows; created a singing telegram company, a consulting company, and a coaching company; married; mothered; trained and taught in places as varied as backroom fitness salons in Slaton, Texas, and overdone McMansion living rooms in Las Vegas. I spent fourteen years going to graduate school when I could fit it in with full-time work. I have written books and authored articles. I shared a speaking venue in India with the Dalai Lama and shared another venue in Argentina with astronaut Buzz Aldrin. I have taught everything from public relations to the history of education at universities from coast to coast and led leadership courses and success seminars. I can honestly tell you, in each endeavor and with each employment, I believed I had the last great job on earth. Every time, every place, every salary, and every 1040. Because within each opportunity and every job, there was a chance and challenge to use it as a platform for purpose, a lectern of learning, and a temple in which to teach. To leave a place or person something better, something more, and something good.

Within each of these various and seemingly random activities, and many more, meeting people from disparate and desperate corners of the globe, I realized that one way or another everyone had made the very same vow I had made in my dorm room, to live a magnificent life full of meaning and to make a positive, meaningful, and enduring impact.

It is clear to me that the unhappiness and despair most people feel comes from spending their days, months, and years in work they feel doesn't matter, in not keeping that internal vow—in not mattering.

Look, we have to work. That's a fact. We are not trust fund babies (most of whom end up in rehab, so take solace), and we have to spend the better part of our days, and eventually our lives, at a job. For forty, fifty, or sixty years. Prime time. Best hours of the day, year in year out.

If you feel insignificant, you will also feel road rage and suffer parental disregard, alcohol and drug abuse, obesity, and/or anxiety, all in the name of quieting that inner yawp of anonymity and impending mortality.

But what if those who can, teach? Those, like you, like me, who believe teaching is the last great job on earth.

Idealistic? Sure.

Simplistic? Maybe.

Possible? Yes.

Becoming a teacher is choosing to participate in the greatness of being. You are giving expression to your convictions. You have chosen one of the few careers labeled a "calling." That I am delighted and excited you have decided to answer.

With reverence, your fellow teacher,

Ronda

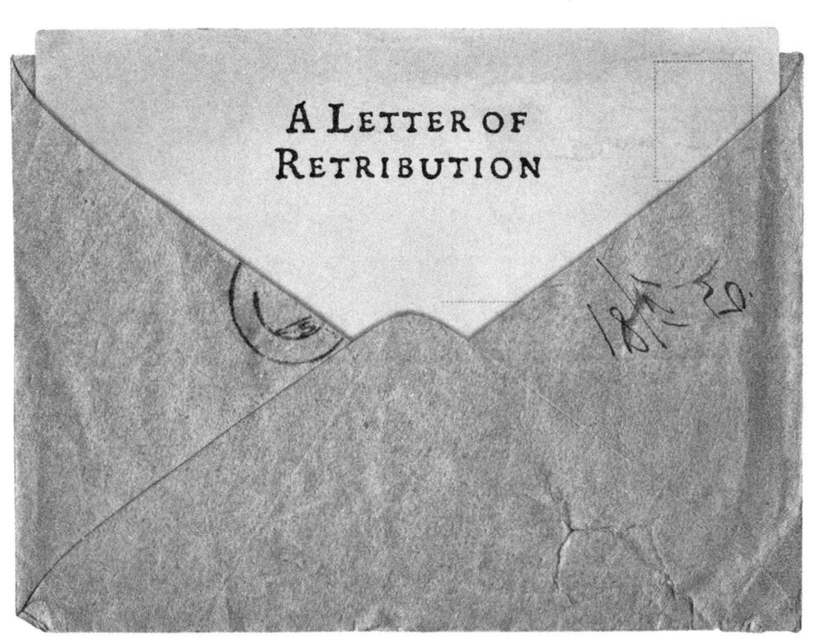
A Letter of Retribution

Is there a heaven, Patrick?

You spent most of your life in hell, so it would only be fair if you landed with angels.

Mother took drugs in a failed attempt to therapeutically abort you, Daddy called you Pinhead, I ignored you, and Marcia, our baby sister, adored you. You were the butt of most of the jokes in our family. Skinny and malnourished in all senses of the word. Only one person showed up for the only birthday party you ever had. You were not gifted in sports, you got the mutilation of acne, and you had a big mouth that got you beat up at school bus stops, fired from jobs, and avoided by most of polite society. You thought of yourself as a badass, but most who knew you just thought you were an ass.

I remember you threw banana peels out your bedroom window in the winter, and the thaw revealed the habit. Daddy found them, brought them to you, and I was never sure what was said or done with them when he stormed into your room. I did hear the words "homeless" and "cretin." Mother was putting away your laundry one morning and found that you had stolen a stereo that was set up in your closet. You had been listening with headphones so no one could hear it but you. You were no criminal genius. I can't say what happened to you when your music stopped, but I heard the scuffling and saw the stereo being hauled to the garage. That same year they found pills of some kind in your drawer and promptly removed you from the swim team, the only extracurricular, legal activity you were involved in.

Here's why I am writing: I never defended you to them or anyone. In fact, I tried hard not to let anyone know you were my brother. I realize that makes me an accomplice to the ongoing assaults and acrimony aimed directly and solely at you by, seemingly, the world. No excuses. I was simply playing the Eddie Haskell to your perceived Charles Manson. And I didn't really like you. I thought you deserved most of the punishment you got. I was also afraid to help you, for fear of getting wrapped up in the hairball that was your life.

For all of our lives together, I believed I had a brother who was mean, twisted, and evil. Drugs, alcohol, and untreated physical and mental health issues led to thefts, all manner of shady business, and honestly just not being a very good person. As much as I understand where your issues come from and have sympathy for that, you made no effort to fix anything and were a jerk pretty much your entire life. The three-year prison sentence for trying to shoot the police who showed up at your house because they thought you had murdered your wife proves my point. I remember wishing you got thirty years behind bars.

When you told me you were going to take me out to the desert and put a bullet in my head, it was one of the few times I believed every word you said. Frankly, I am surprised and grateful that as a family, we didn't end up as a murder/suicide headline.

I can't know, or understand, what went wrong with you. I can only be relieved that you are gone, and I do hope in peace.

You were my brother; we shared DNA and eighteen years under the same roof. I regret what I added to your pain and self-loathing, but you didn't, maybe couldn't, give me any goodness or kindness that would result in any affection for you. I am relieved that you are gone, and I mean it when I say I hope you are in a better place.

And so goodbye, Patrick,

Ronda

A Letter of Stride

Dear Mr. Tillman,

I have seen you walking through the neighborhood many times—always hunched, bundled against the elements, moving slowly but steadily, your hiking boots heavy against the pavement.

You never looked up, never said hello, but I noticed you.

Every morning, as I laced up my running shoes, I thought of you. I admired your persistence, but if I'm being honest, I also celebrated my own youth and agility, my ability to move faster, cover more ground, and push past obstacles with ease. I had no idea, then, how much I would come to learn from your pace.

I started teaching in a hurry. Freshly armed with degrees and accolades, I had something to prove. I dazzled students with my intellectual footwork, raced ahead of them, urged them to catch up, to push harder, and to keep pace with me. But teaching is not about performance. I learned that the hard way the day I ran into a former student—a student I had spent an entire semester with—who didn't remember my name. Worse, I didn't remember hers.

That moment winded me, more than any run ever could. I had assumed teaching was about content and intellectual showmanship, but I had forgotten to connect. And in failing to connect, I had been forgotten. What good were all my awards, my carefully constructed lectures, if I had not made a lasting difference in the lives of my students?

I had been running too fast to see them.

One morning, I rounded the corner of a steep hill and saw you, ahead of me. My music was blasting, my cadence strong, my mind set on passing you. But something—some small voice of knowing—urged me to slow down instead. To meet you at your pace.

So I called out, "Good morning!"

I startled you. You turned, and I saw, for the first time, the scars on your face, the marks of battles fought and survived. I understood, in an instant, why you kept your head down, why you covered yourself so completely. I understood because I had battled the same enemy. Skin cancer had left its mark on me too.

I matched your steps that day, and you told me your name—Luther Tillman. You told me about your walks, your home up the road, and about losing your wife. I listened. And when it was time for our paths to part, I told you I'd see you again.

And then, just as I was putting my headphones back in, I heard you call after me.

"Thanks . . . thanks for talking to me."

Your voice was clearer, your head just slightly higher than before.

I turned, and you were waving.

I walked home with tears welling in my eyes.

You see, Mr. Tillman, you reminded me of the power and promise of being a teacher.

You showed me what I had been missing in my own profession—not the speed, not the knowledge, not the dazzling footwork, but the slowing down. The seeing. The walking beside.

For years, I had been teaching like I had been running—fast, focused on my own ability, my own progress. But the best teaching, the kind that truly matters, happens when we slow down. When we see the people in front of us. When we call out a greeting, offer a hand, meet each other where we are.

Now, after many years in the classroom, I no longer try to outpace my students. I learn all their names, I listen to their stories, I open space for them to bring their whole selves into the room. I invite them to my home, we bake cookies, we take hikes, we talk about life. I take chances, I make mistakes, I model what it means to be human in front of them.

I teach with my whole self now, and in doing so, I have finally earned the honor of being called a teacher and am always stirred when a student says, "Thank you . . . thank you for teaching me."

I don't know if you remember that morning, Mr. Tillman. But I do. And I will always be grateful for what you taught me.

Your student,

Ronda

A Letter of Mortality

Dear Jonathan,

There I was, far from home—an alleged adult, a single mother with two small boys, masquerading as both a professor and a fully functional human. In reality, I was a California oddity, dropped into a Pennsylvania burg. When I walked into my first classroom at the local university, the students assumed I was a secretary sent to explain why their professor was late. That's how much presence I had.

Did I ever tell you about that first day? I did what every pedagogical guidebook suggests—took roll. The first student was from Allentown, so, naturally, I belted out the first line of the Billy Joel song: "Well, we're living here in Allentown . . ." Silence. Blank stares. Not a single chuckle. I pressed on.

Then I came to Dale Lay. I tried not to make eye contact as he said, "Present." The very next name? Kim Lapenas. You can't make this up. I was holding it together until I got to Troy Nipple. At that point, I lost the battle. Looking at all three of them, I asked, "Do you guys hang out together?" The class finally cracked, and that's when I knew: Maybe, just maybe, I'd survive this.

And I did. But not just because that small town wrapped its arms around my boys and me. Not just because I found my footing as an educator. But because I found you. Or more accurately, because you found me.

You loved me into becoming a lifelong friend.

Let's be honest: You were older than I was—not in years but in emotional intelligence, wisdom, humor, and an uncanny ability to make people feel safe, seen, and valued. Who does that at twenty-two? Who counsels their teacher—a woman a decade older—without an ounce of condescension, only genuine care? Other than, say, Emmanuel Macron? (But I digress.)

I'll tell you who: someone who's walked rough roads, who knows what it feels like to go without the love they deserved, and who somehow—somehow—still chooses to be a light. That's you.

Of course, it wasn't an instant friendship. It took time. But I can tell you the exact moment our bond was sealed.

I gave the class a fake pop quiz, pretending to be stern: You haven't done your homework, you don't participate enough, so this quiz will determine your final grade. Silence. Terror. I had them. I passed out the quizzes, face down. "Don't turn them over until I say go."

You, of course, sat in the back. School wasn't exactly your thing. You didn't look at me with respect so much as bemused skepticism, like you were watching a blonde attempt calculus.

Then I said, "Go." The class flipped their quizzes—only to find they were filled with ridiculous, impossible joke questions. Relief washed over them. You? You just shook your head, half admiring, half exasperated.

Not long after, I received a letter from the dean's office, summoning me for a serious discussion about a psychologically damaging prank I had played on my students. Someone had reported me.

I was panicked. I couldn't afford to lose my job. I had two kids to support. To make matters worse, when I received the letter, I was already on campus, dressed in a full gorilla suit—running through the halls to prove to my advertising class that just getting attention isn't enough; there has to be purpose.

So you can imagine my dread. Not only was I about to be reprimanded, but I was going to have to defend myself while dressed as a primate.

I saw you in the hallway, gorilla head under my arm, and you said, "You OK? You look like something's wrong."

I told you about the meeting, and you reassured me, "Don't worry too much. It'll be fine."

I didn't think much more about it—I was too busy hyperventilating.

The appointed hour came. I walked into the dean's office, still in my gorilla suit. No one even blinked. The receptionist greeted me with, "The dean will see you now," as if it were perfectly normal for a faculty member to be dressed as a jungle creature.

The dean—who looked uncannily like Colonel Sanders—stood up and simply said, "I see you must have had an interesting morning."

"I'm so sorry," I stammered. "I didn't have time to change, but I didn't want to be late for this meeting."

He nodded. "Professor Beaman, we must be mindful of our students' mental health. Pranks like this could trigger panic attacks."

"Oh, I know all about panic attacks," I shot back. "I had one when I got your letter."

He was unimpressed. "Let's keep these kinds of jokes to a minimum, shall we?"

"Yes, sir. Absolutely. Never again," I lied.

He dismissed me with a final "You may return to . . . whatever it is you were doing. You do teach communication, not zoology, correct?"

I left the office feeling like my academic career had been brief and undistinguished.

When I reached the lobby, the receptionist walked me to the door—for some reason.

And the second she opened it, there you were—grinning, holding helium balloons and flowers, and laughing your head off. The dean stood behind me, and he was laughing, the receptionist was laughing, and I was crying in relief and respect for the sheer chutzpah of the boy with the balloons.

You had orchestrated the entire thing. You had gotten the dean to sign the letter, warned the receptionist, and pulled off one of the greatest pranks of all time. On behalf of the entire class, you said.

We laughed until we cried. Then you took me to lunch. You admitted you hadn't realized I'd actually panic all morning but insisted, let's be honest—it was worth it. And it was.

That moment cemented our weird and wonderful friendship. You're weird, and I'm wonderful.

I only had that year with you before you graduated. We paddleboarded the Inner Harbor in Baltimore; had so many lunches discussing life, the future, our fathers (*oy!*); saw movies; took the boys hiking and trick-or-treating; and played baseball in my backyard. When our dog ran away, we called you in the middle of the night, and you arrived with flashlights and "dog treats" that looked a lot like bite-size REESE'S Peanut Butter Cups. We dropped the treats throughout the woods in the back of our house Hansel-and-Gretel style so Foozy might follow the trail back to us. The boys were laughing and sneaking some of the treats . . . you made their broken hearts chocolate-covered.

I'm writing instead of calling because I need you to see the words. I need you to hold on to what I am about to share. Knowing you don't like to read, I can only implore you to continue just a bit further.

When, after I'd spent months trying to reach you, you texted, *texted*, that you had almost died from a rare and lethal infection, the news hit me like an internal hurricane running rampant from my throat to my toes. My throat closed, I couldn't breathe, and every one of my organs reeled and whirled. It was as if I had been ill, as if I had suffered, as if I were with you, were you. It was eerie and unsettling, but revelatory.

It was as if your mortality were strangely tangled up with mine. We were meant to be immune from death; our story still had so many chapters and chances to reconnect and create happy endings. But now, I realized—I could lose you. And that thought shook me to my core.

You, my unstoppable friend, survived hundreds of days in a coma. You took on that virus like the high school wrestler you once were. You pinned it. And then, because you never do anything halfway, you got a hand transplant—not just for yourself, but to pave the way for veterans who needed the same.

And I wasn't there.

I didn't know.

I didn't help.

The shock of the story revealed the truth; you had been on my mind from the day we met. And you never left.

I have since watched videos of you, an ABC special done about you learning to jump rope on one leg. I saw you trying to catch tennis balls with a hand that wasn't yours. I saw photos of you with your daughter, your wife, and your life. In the videos and photos, I saw through the successful Hollywood producer and into the soul of the young university student in the last seat in the first row to my right, closest to the window.

I've tried to see you, in more than my memory, but you won't let me. You say you're busy, but I think you don't want me to see you.

But, the joke is on you, Jono; I see you all the time.

I see you in the students I teach—the ones with hidden depths. The ones who don't always let you in right away, yet they welcome you to try. Students with big dreams and the big talent to make them come true. Students who are smarter than they know or ready to help others, generous with their time and talents.

It's possible, of course, you may be right . . . again. That not seeing you means you remain forever in my classroom, the boy laughing at and with me, reminding me that it's not who has the PhD but the degree to which a person connects with you and makes this oftentimes-cold world so much warmer.

Still, I want to see you; I want to touch you and hold your new hand. I want to laugh over lunch, tell our inside jokes, relive that wonderful time when we were young and full of possibilities that never included a virus, my cancer, divorces, and the vagaries of life.

For now, my words, this letter, will have to hold space for the day that may happen. Put it in a drawer and read it every now and then until you are compelled to see an old friend who loves you. Please make it soon.

The clock keeps ticking.

Ronda

A Letter of Hell

Dear Chase,

"Mom, I am lost," you said.

I was instantaneously transported to the days long ago when you liked being lost—and later found—running through grocery stores, taking off on a hike, or burying your nose in a good book. The days when you were just being a boundless boy, unafraid and undaunted by the world around you . . . because you were unaware of the world around you. Back then I was the world, and our home the boundary from which you journeyed. Back then "lost" meant being bewildered about your own whereabouts while believing I would find you. There was safety, security, and abiding love anchored in the temporary and self-designed vanishment.

This morning's "lost" means a totally different thing as you face the middle of your life, doesn't it? Whether you mean feelings of uncertainty about your role in the world, a lack of direction, a persistent unhappiness, or maybe burnout from a job that leaves little time to spark joy, this "lost" is heavy, depressing, and disorienting. And no mama wants to see their child, no matter the age of that child, feeling this way. And no child wants to hear their mother give them platitudes like, "You just need to think positive," or "It's all in your head," and "Think how lucky you are compared to other people."

What's a mother, this mother—the queen of the platitudes "This too shall pass" and "Buck up"—to do? What words are available to me to be of some succor?

I remember my dad telling me, "You have never thought, done, felt, experienced, or said anything that I didn't think, do, feel, or say when I was your age." Man, that was annoying at best and, at worst, true! As I got older, I realized what he meant.

Keep in mind, this was the same guy who when driving with me down a dead-end road, high above the ocean, said, "Sometimes I feel like I should just put my foot on the gas and keep going."

There is a sameness to being human, within reason, and a trajectory, a stage, or whatever you want to call it to what we all must go through to live a life. And oh, the mundanity.

I think that is the key—the being able to triumph through the mundane—to living the beauty in the effort of each day. I am trying here not to be too platitudinous, but words are so small for expressing the privilege, promise, and pain of living.

This letter, my words, my heart, and love may not be able to solve your current sense of despair, but what about a word or two from Dante?

Do you remember reading Dante's *Inferno* in high school? *Abandon all hope, ye who enter* . . . he essentially warned us that midway upon the journey of our life is a pivotal moment of introspection and self-evaluation. He finds himself . . . wait for it . . . *lost* in a dark forest, symbolizing the uncertainties and challenges of midlife. You're in good company, Chase, part of the divine comedy.

Here's where I will end, as did Dante, leaving you in this middle of your life, feeling lost, temporarily in the darkness, promising you that like Dante, you, too, will once again see stars.

Those stars are your sons, your wife, your brother, your parents, and your friends. You will be illuminated by the people you have helped, the impact you have had, the pleasures, talents, and rewards given to you. Glimpse your life through the telescope of your heart and be overwhelmed by the sheer galactic rapture of finding yourself loved. Use that love as your compass, and you will find you are no longer lost—you are home.

From a little spark may burst a flame,
Mother

A Letter of Discovery

Dear Loving, Loyal, Lucky, Luminous, Letter-Worthy Lander . . .

You are graduating from high school and leaving this summer.

There is so much in that sentence. Yet I find myself at a loss for words that could come close to the emotions within that sentence. I have not come around to saying that you are leaving out loud. It's like saying it makes it real, and I don't want it to be real . . . but then again, I do. It's your turn. You are itching for the adventures to come, for the life you will build, and the world you will live in. That's how it should be, but still, I cry at my loss for my soon-emptier world and the smaller world I will live in with you gone.

I remember when you were born. I thought, "Well, I can never love him as much as I loved my own babies." I don't do anything small, and being wrong is no exception. I remember the moment our relationship changed like it was yesterday. Your mom and dad went out on a date, and I was babysitting you. You were asleep in your portable crib, inside my closet. I tiptoed in to make sure you were OK . . . I stood above you, looking down into the crib. You were wearing a fuzzy little onesie, your hot, oversize Charlie Brown head was sweaty, and your hair was matted to the back of your head . . . and *love* hit me like a thunderbolt. I thought, "I would lay down my life for this child." To this day I would, but please don't test this.

And did I mention, you are leaving this summer? To commence, challenge, and create your future. To become a good man.

Trying to learn to be a good man is like learning to play volleyball against a wall. Clever how I threw in one of your favorite sports. Anyway, you are only a good man—a competent, capable, interesting, and lovable man—when you're doing it for, or with, other people. And that is what I have seen you do so far, helping others become better, taking on challenges that help you grow, being a kind and patient big brother and loving son. This is groundwork for greatness.

Once more I write, you are leaving this summer. It still stabs. I shall have lost the boy I loved so well but perhaps shall find the man I shall love even more. I hope you come visit often and come through the front door without knocking. I hope you head to the kitchen for a snack and slump on the sofa to share YouTubes or to talk anime. I hope you come in and feel the weight of adulthood leave you for those visits and moments. I promise cookies that will be almost as fresh as my curiosity about all things Lander.

I never dreamed of being a grandmother, I never dreamed we would be such a part of each other's lives, I never dreamed I would see you grow up day by day, year by year . . . which only goes to show that many of the gifts you will receive in life are unexpected, bigger than you can dream, will hit you like thunderbolts, and are worth laying down your life for; take my word for it.

I love you,
Gogo

A LETTER OF ELEVATION

Dear Kili,

From the moment I first heard your name—Kili—I knew you were destined to be someone remarkable. Named after the shining mountain your dad climbed while your mom carried you, you came into the world with quiet strength, steady grace, and a soul that feels a little older than your years. Just like Kilimanjaro, you don't demand attention—you simply rise with dignity and presence, letting your actions speak for you.

Being the middle child isn't always easy, but you've made it into an art form—easygoing, thoughtful, and quietly determined. You don't seek the spotlight, but you shine in your own way: like Gary Cooper in those old black-and-white films—cool, calm, and deeply kind.

One day you said to me, "It doesn't cost anything to be kind," and I've never forgotten it. That simple truth tells me everything about your character. You live your values. You show up. You care. Whether it was helping me lead the Branch Out Club or handing out snacks to the younger kids with that sweet focus of yours—you weren't just doing tasks; you were building community.

And then there was that school project, the one where you could have picked anyone famous for your *People* magazine cover, and you chose . . . me. You drew me. You wrote about my enthusiasm and love for people. Kili, that was one of the greatest honors of my life. You saw me. And you reminded me how important it is to be seen through the eyes of someone who knows your heart.

I've loved watching you grow—not just taller or wiser, but into someone who appreciates the beauty of a first-class trip, the elegance of a well-cut jacket, and the thrill of Formula One racing. You've got style, kid. But more importantly, you've got soul.

As you keep working toward your dreams—college, travel, the next race or adventure—remember this: You already are someone important. Not because of grades or awards or recognition, but because of your gentle spirit, your thoughtfulness, and the way you quietly make the world better just by being in it.

You are my shining mountain.

With love that knows no summit,

Gogo

A Letter of Roots

Dear Jet,

You and I met on the day you were born. The memory may be a bit hazy for you, but I recall every detail. The copper-colored hair, the gray-green eyes were familiar to me. In fact, I have a photo of you being held by my mother, your great-grandmother, just days before she passed. She is looking off in the distance—her copper-colored hair and gray-green eyes fixed on the horizon she was facing. You were the last person she held. And then, you took hold of me.

Not even your mother or dad could explain the instant, unbreakable bond we had. Upon seeing me, you would reach your arms out, your face would light up, and cries of despair and desperate reaching would follow when I had to pass you back to your parents. It didn't take long before I started calling you my FHB—my Favorite Human Being. It just fit. You filled up the quiet places in my life with joy and laughter. You made ordinary moments sparkle. And without even trying, you taught me that love doesn't end when someone leaves us—it grows in new directions.

It's one of the strangest and most profound things about family—how pieces of people we may have never known, or only knew in passing, find their way into you. A crooked smile, a fierce streak of determination, a love of words or rhythm—traits passed down like secret messages from ancestors whose names you might never hear. Watching you grow, I see flickers of not only my mother but also your maternal great-great-grandfather's Irish humor, your uncle's talent, maybe even a stubborn tilt of the chin that once belonged to someone we only know from black-and-white photos. This inheritance—both beautiful and bewildering—is part of the mire and mess of family. It connects us in ways we don't always understand, reminding us that we are not just ourselves but also echoes of all those who came before.

We both are loud and boisterous, love telling a good story, and never miss a chance to find the limelight. You sat by me at dinners, plays, movies, and on the couch when I read *All Creatures Great and Small* to the family on Sunday evenings. We couldn't get enough of each other.

Do you remember the vintage dinner bells we had on the table? The rule was if you picked one up, you had to make a toast. Well, you would ring those bells multiple times, and your salute was usually a laugh, an emphatic "hello," or just a funny face. The more the family applauded, the more Jet Toasts we got! When I was writing one of my books, I received a video your mother took of you writing a book. Our hair was thick and crazy, and we said it was our hair-itage! I was moved to tears to spy you practicing dance moves to try out for a play, remembering the days I would hide and practice for cheerleading tryouts.

Jet—like your name, I knew the day would come when you would have to take off, at supersonic speed. Teenage now, and I don't see you as often, or as carefree. That's OK. Teenagers are supposed to grow apart a bit—to stretch and explore and begin to define themselves in new ways. That's how it should be. But even as you grow into your own person, I hope for the day you come once more and tell me about your life, your loves, your dreams, and your disappointments—because I am here for all of it. I am here for you.

You are kind, curious, and full of wonder. I see in you a beautiful mix of old soul and new spirit. And I see in myself the very best version of who I am—because of you.

And you remain, now and always, my FHB.

With all my love,
GoGo

A Letter of Acknowledgment

Dear Seanshine,

From the very beginning, your timing was as sharp as a comedian in top form, the punch line landing with perfect precision at almost ten pounds. You literally had me in stitches—sixteen of them, to be exact.

I had just indulged in a Labor Day feast, savoring sticky barbecue ribs and a slice of blueberry pie so large it could have doubled as a flotation device, when the first labor pain struck. And true to your nature, you made your debut on Labor Day itself—because of course you did. You've been hitting your cues with effortless brilliance ever since.

You arrived as a big baby with an even bigger presence, a head full of hair the same color as your ruddy, newborn face, and the kind of neck control that made you look like you'd been rehearsing this role for months. When the doctor gave you the traditional welcome slap, I swear you hit him back.

Combative and clever, you had a flair for the dramatic—a grand heart wrapped in a grand personality. You were the boy who plucked dandelions for me as if they were the rarest of roses, who, at five years old, stood like a pint-size guardian, determined to protect me, always reminding me that I was beautiful, and that you were proud of me. Our bond, woven through both stormy trials and sunlit moments, has always been unshakable.

From the dandelion days to the moment I spotted you at the end of the stadium tunnel after my doctorate ceremony, standing alone in a golden halo of sunlight, bouquet in hand, waiting for me with a quiet, knowing smile—your presence has always been my constant. Through care, comfort, and comedy, you have been, and always will be, one of my greatest joys.

Lately, I've been reflecting on the moments that stand out—not just the big ones, but the quiet, unexpected ones. The ones that, in their simplest form, reveal the essence of you.

It was you. At just five years old, sitting cross-legged on the floor, handily beating a room full of graduate students at Trivial Pursuit. The laughter, the disbelief, the sheer delight on your face as you answered question after question.

Smart.

It was you. At the Earth Day celebration, suddenly breaking into a backspin—a *backspin!*—on the pavement. I didn't even know you could breakdance, but there you were, center stage, as a circle of strangers gathered around to cheer. **Fun.**

It was you. The one who ran straight into your older brother's fight on the playground, shirt torn, face streaked with mud, fists flying. You didn't hesitate. You stood beside him, took the hit, and came home bruised but unwavering.

"No one messes with my brother," you said. **Loyal.**

It was you. The night of the Pinewood Derby, when you were certain you had won—until you found out you hadn't. We sat in the car, sunroof open to the night sky, sorting through what it all meant. You were hurting, but even at seven years old, you wrestled with a truth most people spend a lifetime avoiding: There will always be someone better, but there will also always be those who never get the chance. That night, we decided that being kind is what makes a person a real winner. And I still believe we were right. **Virtuous.**

It was you. The year my face bore the scars of skin cancer surgery, the year you saw my fear and felt it as if it were your own. You sobbed harder than I did. You turned my face toward you and whispered reassurances I didn't know I needed. You didn't turn away. **Empathetic.**

It was you. Still in high school, standing in front of four hundred students in my education class, guitar in hand, voice steady, singing "Fake Plastic Trees," by Radiohead. The room fell silent. You owned the moment. I barely held it together as I whispered, "Wow." Not for the first time. Not for the last. **Talented.**

It was you. At one of my student gatherings, standing in the corner with a lampshade on your head, committing to the bit with an unshakable seriousness that only made it funnier. Thirty minutes later, you were still there. **Hilarious.**

Being your mother has been an unrivaled experience.

A front-row seat to watching a zygote become an *unequaled, unmatched* human who shines.

And what a joy it is to witness you, every day, becoming more and more *you.*

As a husband, a father, a professor, you have kept your soul alive, your humor intact, and your intellect wide and ranging.

The best part? Every twist and turn—every role, every stage, every punch line—led you exactly where you were meant to be.

Your life is proof that success isn't linear, and timing is about more than just showing up—it's about knowing how to own the moment.

And that, my son, is exactly what you've always done.

So proud to be your mother,

Me

A Letter of Cheer

Dear Sydney,

Two bits, four bits, six bits, a dollar
I say Sydney is my favorite granddaughter!

Yes, I know, you are my only granddaughter, but still, I think you would remain my favorite even if there were competition. As your grandmother, I hope to give you unconditional love, guidance, wisdom, support, and all things grandmotherly, like cookies, hugs, sharing family history, and . . .

Cheerleading.

Let me tell you why.

In junior high, high school, and college, donning my cheer sweater embroidered with my name on the sleeve was not simply about high jumps or splits. Cheerleading for me was about being someone other people counted on to inspire them, to get them excited, to help them win. I relished every routine, every assembly, all the summer cheer camps, and the positive public persona we were expected to project. I loved it all. Except the splits. I never liked or could do the splits.

With every "Victory! Victory! Is our cry, V-I-C-T-O-R-Y," I knew what my mission on earth was and why I was born: to be cheerful, to greet all equally, to be peppy and encouraging, and to be a jumping, yelling, rhyming, clapping, pom-pomming role model of enthusiasm, spirit, and *pep*!

Now, I can't tell you how many people, including those in my own family, made fun of cheerleading or worse, saying it was not doing women's roles in society any favors. But let me tell you this: When I was a girl, no one would have voted for a female student body president; cheerleading was the only route available to be a leader. I know what you're thinking . . . prehistoric. However, despite strides in women's representation in powerful roles, a surprising number of people across the world still don't trust women to lead effectively. These biases are deep-seated—and difficult to change. Cheer teaches you to accept defeat gracefully, be proud of success, and maintain respect for fellow competitors or teams no matter a game's outcome, and that applies on a court or field and in an office or boardroom.

It's important to look at the world and circumstances into which you were born and instead of complaining about the unfairness of it, get off your "*but*" and blaze trails toward what and who you want to be. There have always been and will always be girls and women who were told, "*But* girls can't play football" or "*But* women can't run a corporation or country" or "*But* cheerleading is girls cheering for boys rather than doing something themselves."

But Sydney, I wanted to cheer, and I didn't think anything like that . . . I wanted to be a leader, I wanted to help others and share my enthusiasm for school—for participating instead of sitting on the sidelines—and I wanted to do something that was physical, strong, and demanding, plus be part of a team. Cheerleading helped develop my self-confidence and self-worth. Cheerleading taught me discipline and how to work toward goals, to be responsible and determined.

The many and varied roads my life has taken, including appearing on television shows, being a university professor, writing books, becoming a fitness guru, and more, have all been related to being a cheerleader and putting myself out front in the world. Sydney, I came here to live out loud. And to cheer others on to do the same. Especially you.

Cheer isn't for the weak of heart or spine. Life will knock the wind out of you from time to time. It will take your cheer and squeeze it, stomp on it, and try to destroy it. People may boo, some will cheat, many of the rules in life will seem unfair. I want to share with you that the world doesn't care if you lose your hope, your dreams, or your cheer. The world just keeps going on without you. You have to care, and you have to "Go, fight, win!"

No matter whom you become or what you decide to do, remember you have cheerleader DNA! It's much easier to look at the world and see what is wrong and wear it. There will never be a shortage of pessimists. To see the discouraged and be the type of person who thinks, "I can help this situation, I can solve this problem, I can help others get through this; I remain undaunted" is much tougher, but also heroic, intelligent, strong, and optimistic. Cheer, under any circumstance, would be the best legacy I can leave you.

Live your life with grace and grit; practice your routines daily; remember that you are part of a squad, not a solo; and don't agonize over missteps, let losses linger, or laud your wins. Give smiles generously, don't agonize over harsh calls from people who only sit in the stands and watch, and no matter how high you jump, strive to stick your landing.

I will always and forever be cheering for you,

Gogo

A Letter of Genius

Dear Merrick,

From the very moment you arrived in this world, it was clear you were something special. And now, at the grand age of seven, you are already a force to be reckoned with—part mathematician, part comedian, part walking library, and, of course, a devoted penguin enthusiast.

I thought at first you didn't like me. I think it was the screaming every time I tried to hug you that tipped me off. But now I know it was just a huge brain trapped in a small head, trying desperately to make sense of the world of big people, big noises, and grandmothers who show up from out of nowhere and want kisses and hugs.

I am glad I have finally grown on you.

I love the way your mind works: how you see patterns in numbers the way others see shapes in the clouds, how you memorize every word in every book in your classroom as if the words have found a permanent home inside you. I love how you make me laugh, how you understand the magic of a well-placed punch line or a funny face. And, of course, I love how much you love penguins—because really, what's not to love about a bird that wears a tuxedo everywhere it goes?

One day, you might grow up to be a mathematician who finds new numbers no one has discovered yet. Or a scientist who studies penguins in the wild and learns how to speak their secret language. Or maybe an author who writes stories that other kids will memorize. Or maybe—just maybe—you'll be something no one has even imagined yet. Dinosaur DNA builder? Mars colony architect? Creator of a brand-new instrument? A linguist who can really talk to all animals? The world is waiting, and I believe you will deliver.

Whatever path you take, I want you to know this: I will always delight in who you are. Not because of what you accomplish (though I know it will be great), not just because of how brilliant you are (though that is undeniable), but because of the way you see the world—with wonder, with humor, with kindness. Because of the way your eyes light up when you learn something new, the way you make people laugh at just the right moment, the way you care about the things (and creatures—especially penguins!) that matter to you. I delight in you because you are you—curious, clever, full of life—and my world is better because you let me in yours.

With all my love,
GoGo

A Letter of Capacity

Dear Mr. Fallon,

Since you and I were partners on your *Password* show, can I call you Jimmy?

I appreciate you asking me to be on *The Tonight Show* after we met, and I want to explain why I repeatedly declined.

I was supposed to be famous too.

At least I thought so for most of my childhood. The world is only missing out on me because I never learned to do anything with my imagined, but insistent, talents. I tried, on many occasions, to be discovered, and I started with my toughest audience, my parents.

In the second grade, I asked my dad for dancing lessons.

"No, we can't afford that."

"But, Daddy, I have it all figured out. It costs thirty-five cents for each pack of Lucky Strikes, almost two dollars for a bottle of Green Stripe Scotch, and that's the five dollars a week I need to pay for my lessons. If you gave up Scotch and cigarettes, I could dance. And you would be a lot healthier."

"That's an impressive argument. I applaud your efforts. But let's say I give up these things that I enjoy very much and get run over by a truck—what fun would I have had? Besides, if I gave up both Scotch and smoking, I wouldn't be a very happy daddy, no matter how good you danced . . . so no."

I let a week go by, and I asked again.

"Daddy, how about voice lessons?"

"You still on this kick?"

"Show business is my life. Please?"

And that's when I got my first audition . . . for my parents.

Now, the thing is, when I was growing up, I had no idea what happened in other houses. So I took my dad's request in stride, figuring everyone who wanted singing lessons had to try out for the folks.

"Before you earn the right to have lessons, we need to hear you sing. I would like you to prepare two songs for tonight. Mother and I will listen, and then we will decide about lessons," he replied, hoping I wouldn't take the bait and proving he didn't know me too well.

"Great! What time tonight?" I clapped and chirped.

"We'll call for you around seven."

They'll call for me? Where was I going to be? I didn't exactly have a music room to retire to, and our house was under a thousand square feet. No matter, off I went to the room I shared with my sister to practice. I had less than four hours; that would be two hours for each song. Minus some time for costume choice and choreography.

For the remainder of the afternoon, I worked on my big number, "Sunny," by Bobby Hebb. My rendition was two minutes and forty-four seconds of Arizona suburb soul. It was sure to be a showstopper. My parents would be so amazed by my songstress stylings, I would only have to do another number because they wouldn't be able to get enough.

At the appointed hour, cocktail time, I did get "the call." My brother and sister, hoping it was dinner, walked down the hall with me. My dad, still in his suit, welcomed us into the living room and suggested that my siblings view the audition from the hallway. I proceeded past them, every inch the star I was sure to be after tonight.

My mother was already seated, holding a clipboard. A clipboard? My dad took his seat next to her, grabbed a legal pad, swilled his Scotch on the rocks, and said:

"Ronda, what will be your first song?"

"I will be performing 'Sunny.'"

Both parents scribbled something on their notes; both my brother and sister were giggling in the hallway.

"Please, begin."

I cleared my throat, smiled, and with all my heart, belted out the song.

Sunny, yesterday my life was filled with rain.
Sunny, you smiled at me and really eased the pain.

I was building up to the chorus, complete with sweeping and open arms:

You gave to me your all and all.

Now I feel ten feet tall.

Sunny one so true, I love you.

Deep breath, here came the finale . . .

"Ronda, you can stop right there," said my dad.

"Huh?"

"Stop there."

More note writing. My brother and sister were backing away slowly.

"Do you have something else?"

"Something, ah, else?" I stammered.

"Yes, another number?"

I didn't like the way this was going. I could feel my ears getting hot, my stomach starting to churn.

"Maybe they just want to make sure being so good at 'Sunny' wasn't a fluke," I feebly reasoned.

"I have a Troggs song," I said queasily.

"Go ahead."

I got through the first three lines of "Love Is All Around."

I feel it in my fingers, I feel it in my toes. [Pointing at toes, classy touch, I thought.] Well, love is all around me, and so the feeling grows.

"OK, thank you—that's it."

"That's it?" I questioned.

"That's it?" I thought. Was this an "I get my lessons, that's it?" Or was it an "I am more than you thought I was, that's it?" Was it an "I stunned you?" What was "That's it"?

"Yes," my dad repeated, "That's it—that's all we need. Mother and I will have a meeting tonight after dinner and tell you in the morning what we have decided."

I was too excited by the prospects of something big happening in my life to sleep. I got up early the next morning, dressed for school, gathered my books, and set the breakfast table, humming all the while, imagining telling my friends my news about singing lessons.

Eventually everyone but my dad was at the table. I was eating my Alpha-Bits when he walked in and sat down.

"Good morning," I said, sharing my "This is going to be *big*" smile.

"Good morning."

"Well, Daddy, what do you think?"

"Ronda, your mother and I talked about this a long time. People who become famous singers have very distinctive voices. People like Lena Horne, Barbra Streisand, Frank Sinatra—you know who they are the minute you hear them. You don't have a voice like that. You have an ordinary voice. You would never make it as a singer. So no, Ronda. We don't think you should waste your time or our money on voice lessons."

Hot ears, churning stomach again, I instantly felt heavy and too slow to argue. I wanted to spell out something nasty with my alphabet cereal, but I just swallowed it all.

Which was worse, I wondered, as I walked to school. Feeling this bad . . . or being ordinary?

Finally, when I was in the eighth grade, for my thirteenth birthday, my parents gave me a tambourine. After I opened it and held it up, my dad laughed and told me to knock myself out.

And I did.

I knocked at every door, every opportunity, and I took on life as a knock-down, drag-out event. I never just knocked around; I worked to be the best at whatever I took on. America's Most Creative Family, National Art of Teaching Award, Top Ten Outstanding Women in America, and so on.

I have done audition after audition, job interview upon job interview, speech after speech, and performances of some kind for all my life . . . and I have been awarded and rewarded many times over for my efforts, applauded, and acknowledged on a global scale, and as Elton John said recently about his retirement, "I don't need more applause."

The reality is that I never recovered from that first audition and spent too much of my life trying to have other people approve of or like me. I am tired of trying. And I didn't even know this until I made the final cut after auditioning for *Password*. I spent fourteen hours with the other contestants prepping for the show with no food or water for over twelve of those hours. The NBC page finally came in and asked, "Who's hungry?" We were too weak to answer and followed him outside, blinking at the sunlight, and trudging toward the food. There, in the distance, was tri-tip barbecue, champagne on ice, and a salad bar. *Mecca*! "This is more like it," I thought as I picked up the pace and headed toward the buffet, trying not to drool. Suddenly a hand grabbed me from behind and spun me around. I was face-to-too-close-face with the page, who said, "This isn't for you; this is for the celebrities. The ordinary people are farther down the street."

Ordinary, once again.

So you see, flying to NYC, sitting in a greenroom with celebrities, and getting verification of being ordinary is something I have finally outgrown.

That night in the living room, my parents taught me that struggle, setback, and losing can be the highest form of song. It has been the sour notes that led me to become extraordinary and, yes, famous where it really matters, in my own life.

Thank you for the invite to appear on your show, for seeing something special in me, and for giving me the reminder, at long last, to realize that I am enough. It's unbelievable how enough I am!

If Hugh Jackman had been a guest on the same show, I might have changed my mind,

Ronda

A Letter of
Admiration

My Mother,

I still remember the cold hum of that cramped doctor's office, the fluorescent lights buzzing louder than the words I was about to hear. I stared at your CAT scan, blinking hard through faucets of tears. I never knew that knees actually do go out and steadied myself, holding on to the exam table. The moment was surreal reality, *Keeping Up with the Kardashians*, *Real Housewives*, or *Survivor* times a million.

The young oncologist was calm. The scene, like his job, was a rerun—scripted with words like "cancer," "Stage 4," "eight months to a year," "so sorry," and "We'll do what we can."

You, of course, were the star of the show—gazing dispassionately at the display of your ravaged insides, deserving of an Emmy for your portrayal of the heroic patient who would triumph.

"I will treat you as if you were my own mother," the doctor said, gently putting his arm around you.

"I'd rather have you treat me like I was your girlfriend," you replied, lifting your chin, leaning into his hug, batting your eyelashes, and smiling. "I think I'll get better care that way."

And that was you—committing to your metastases with the same grace, bravery, humor, and singular devotion with which you committed to your marriage. You had played the role of beautiful wife for over fifty years. As a recent widow, you were adrift—but not lost. You faced your diagnosis the way you faced life: with grit and eyeliner.

"I cry alone," you whispered during the interminable drive back to your downsized modular home—crammed with your oversize furniture and personality.

You never once bemoaned your fatal fate, never let us glimpse self-pity. You wore full makeup and bright clothes every single day you had remaining. You planted perennials. You told me, delighted, "This death sentence means bye-bye budget. I can buy two lipsticks at once if I want."

We shopped for shoes, and I bought you a pair of blue suede UGG boots. It was a tough sell. You were distressed that I didn't want you in heels anymore, those heels Daddy once said made your legs look best. "I think they call them UGGs because they are UGGly," you scoffed. "I don't want to become dowdy," you told me. Six months left to live, at best, and you were concerned about becoming frumpy.

One morning, the call came. "I'm dying," you said. "Come get me. Take me to the emergency room."

I rushed over to find you standing in your driveway—wearing your full-length mink coat over silk pajamas and those UGG boots. Pale as paper, cigarette in hand.

"It's a Lucky Strike," you moaned as I helped you into the car. "A Lucky Strike! If that doesn't make me an oxymoron . . . maybe just a moron."

Turns out the radiologist had failed to warn you that weekly treatments would cause constipation. Stoic as you were glib, and on a daily morphine patch, you simply thought not going to the bathroom for two weeks was a time-saving bonus.

The ER doctor sent you into immediate surgery for fecal impaction.

"You're not the first to tell me I'm full of shit," you told the surgeon before they put you under to remove eight pounds of waste.

Later, in your hospital room, you told me you'd asked to see what had been removed.

"What? Why would you—? Oh, geezus, Mother!" I sputtered.

"It had a little face," you said. "Even little hairs."

I burped a bit of vomit.

"I named it Joey."

My head snapped toward you. We locked eyes. And in that moment, all the absurdities of life and death, cancer, mothers and daughters, indignities, triumphs, legacies, and loss—everything—reached a crescendo. And we laughed. Deep, raucous, and healing laughter.

From then on, anyone rude to us was a "Joey." We decided the whole damn cancer, and everything that came with it, was one giant pile of "Joey."

A day could be a Joey.

Sooner than the diagnosis predicted, you were gone. The cancer had spread into your spine and brain, bypassing only your funny bone.

None of us know what will get us in the end. It'll be a Joey of some kind. All I can do is hope that when my time comes, I can honor what you taught me: to face it with humor, to give pain a waggish name, and to leave behind the legacy of a good laugh.

You never knew this, and I don't know that I ever told you, but I admired you. A bride at seventeen, mother at eighteen, so many lifelong dreams never fulfilled, and you forged on. To your dying day, you remained quintessentially you. Lovely and loving when you wanted to be, a hard case when you had to be. Books are generally not written about people like you, quietly going about what you need to do without drama or histrionics, yet the world is filled with quiet souls who set examples and share courage.

You taught me that life isn't about avoiding pain—it's about showing up for it, fully dressed, lashes curled, and with a memorable comeback ready. I carry that with me. Every. Single. Day.

Your girl, mascara-streaked and smiling,

Ronda

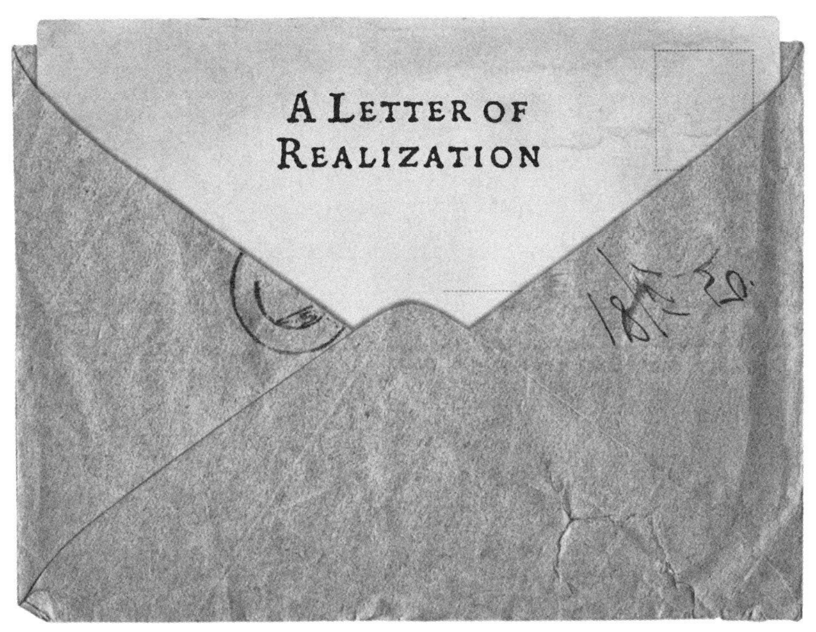

A Letter of Realization

Dear Daddy,

You never liked being called Father. Said it sounded smug. So here I am, near the end of this book, writing my most difficult letter—not to a "father" but to you. Daddy.

I would, in fact, call author and motivational speaker Dale Carnegie my father.

You gave me his book *How to Win Friends and Influence People* after our third or fourth move when I was in fourth grade and complained about having to start all over again at another new school. You told me, "This book will help you understand that it's not about being anyone's friend; you live in a way they should want to be yours." Huh? I was ten. And tired of always being the new kid in school.

Being the dutiful and adoring daughter I was as a child, I read the book cover to cover. In reading Earl's homilies and self-help directives, I came to the unavoidable conclusion that Earl was raising me. I always thought the stories you told, the behaviors you taught, and the sayings you shared were from you . . . but they were all right there in the book. Earl had been raising me all along! The chapters covered all the things you and Earl had taught me:

- "Do This and You'll Be Welcome Anywhere"
- "A Simple Way to Make a Good First Impression"
- "An Easy Way to Become a Good Conversationalist"
- "How to Make People Like You Instantly"

Was that your blueprint for parenting? Was it easier to teach strategy than intimacy? Was it easier to give a gift than to give a hug?

I think maybe it was. Maybe you didn't know how to offer warmth without a gesture to mask it or a joke to deflect it. Maybe, in some ways, you were an emotional cripple—strong in body, quick in mind, but limping in the places where tenderness lives.

It's taken me a long time to sit down and write this. I've dreaded it—not because I don't have things to say but because I have so many. It's the most difficult letter in my book, *A Life in Letters*, and it goes to the daddy who shaped and scarred so much of that life—for better, and for worse.

When I was little, I thought you were the most extraordinary person alive. You were funny—razor-sharp funny—handsome, athletic, charismatic, and undeniably the center of every room. I admired you. I wanted to be like you. I thought you could do no wrong.

But you could. And you did.

I cannot eat any seafood because the night Mother served scallops, which I was happily eating, I asked, "What are these?"

You said, "They're fish eyeballs. Now be quiet and finish up."

I am sure you didn't grasp how dramatic a kid I was, but that night in bed I imagined fish eyeballs, biting into the texture, the taste, and made myself sick to the point of dry heaves.

I leave my shirts untucked, self-conscious that my rear end is two axe handles wide, like you said when I modeled my rodeo-day outfit in eighth grade.

The time you told my Polish boyfriend in high school he was stupid like all Poles, my college boyfriend he was spineless, or my husband he was a coward. You asked how I could get so ugly in just twelve years and said I had hands like Igor in *Frankenstein*.

On and on, Daddy—the barbs, the insults, and the jabs that you masqueraded as jokes.

You had a way of belittling the people closest to you, making your humor a weapon cloaked in charm. It took me a long time to understand that laughing with you often meant laughing at someone we loved. Sometimes, it meant laughing at ourselves. And we learned to do that, because being laughed at without joining in hurt even more. Your jokes left bruises we carried long after the laughter died.

My brother and sister, your son and other daughter, never really recovered from your brand of regard. They both became unhappy alcoholics, dead before their time. I believe at the core of their struggle was the deep, aching sense that they were never quite enough for you. Not seen, not valued, not truly loved for who they were—not unless they performed, reflected you, and amused you. Being called Pinhead all your life, like my brother, or infantilized like my sister, led to some dire consequences—drugs, alcohol, multiple marriages, you name it—yet you never saw or believed you had a part in their misery. They never won friends or influenced anyone; they simply lived in a melancholy disguised as fatherly love.

I took a different route: overachieved, overperformed, and overwrought. Dancing as fast as I could, buddy-buddy with you for the longest time because I believed being on your side was the best bet. The Ron and Ronda Show! I adored you and wanted nothing more than to make you proud. At any cost. Including the loss of respect or relationship with my siblings.

And Mother. She thought you hung the moon, picked you over any of the kids' needs, and even after you cheated, she stayed. You cheated, and she stayed. Because she had no skills and no way out, and because she'd tied her entire life to you when she was just seventeen. But she also loved you, real love, true love, a feeling you may not have ever really experienced.

Once, when I asked her why she always seemed to shrink in your presence, she said, quietly, "Because I've spent my whole life standing in his shadow."

I can't think of anything more heartbreaking—or more true.

Yet, Daddy, now with you gone, I have attempted to understand, comprehend, and attend to who you were and why. And look for the brave parts, the good parts, and the best parts of you as a man, beyond being my father . . . sorry, daddy.

I have learned terms for your behavior—narcissist, sociopath, and others—but I think more of it was living the wrong life and not knowing how to handle the daily distress of what you might have been.

I understand what I couldn't until I became a parent myself: It must have been unimaginably hard to become a father at seventeen. To walk away from your basketball scholarship at Kansas State. To send me to college, giving me the advantages you relinquished. Like many teenage dads, you could have abandoned us, the responsibilities, the death of your own dreams, but you never did. You worked. Repo man, banker, and car salesman. You provided. You moved us from house to house—over thirty of them—chasing jobs, chasing stability, and chasing something you never quite caught. You made sure we had what we needed to survive, even if we didn't always feel seen or valued in the getting of it. In other words, with time and age, I get that you did what you could, what was expected, and that doing so may have burned the fuel that feeds a tender heart.

My drive to lead, to perform, and to shine is part of what saved me from the same outcome. I was in my thirties before I finally broke free from the gravitational pull of your approval and started living my own life. But I had the strength to do that because of the foundation you laid. The discipline, the ambition, the sense that I could walk into a room and make something happen—that came from you.

I carry some of your flaws—your need to be seen, to get credit, to measure too much by appearances. But I also carry your strength. Your charisma. Your grit. And your sense of possibility. I carry the parts of you I'm proud of. And I carry others I've learned to lay down.

You're gone now. And I don't carry the lack, the wistfulness, the desire to have had a daddy who held my hand, who smiled when I entered a room, who was able to love wholeheartedly. I don't want to keep sorting through old scenes trying to rewrite the ending. Instead, I will carry forward the memory of the kind of love you could share, the broken places you healed to hang on, and how amazing it felt when you did shine my way.

This letter isn't about settling scores. It's about setting down the burden. I loved you, Daddy. I learned from you. And now, at last, I've learned how to let go of the parts that no longer serve me or your memory and to hang on tightly to what made me someone I am proud of: a daughter who smiles about being a chip off the old block.

Thank you for the foundation. Thank you for the fight. And thank you, in whatever way you knew how, for loving me.

Love, your namesake and the daughter who shares the best of you,

Ronda

A Letter of Imagining

Dear Me,

Everyone writes letters to their younger selves—let's be original and write one to your older self. No one else is going to do it. All your family has passed away, each of them before they had a chance to be old. This is foreign territory, and I want you to be ready.

I want you to be as involved, interested, and interesting as you have always been—if I do say so myself. I hope your mind still crackles with curiosity and your heart still swells at the sight of a sunrise or waves from kids on a school bus. I hope you have given yourself the grace to slow down—to be stopped in your tracks by the color of a flower, to linger over a well-told story, and to listen fully and deeply to the voices that still surround you. Take the time to look deeply into the eyes of those you encounter, to see reflected back at you all the fears, challenges, sorrows, joys, and fortitude it takes to wear this mortal coil. Connect by asking questions and listening while keeping your own answers short. Don't fall for that "getting invisible" nonsense—you came here to live out loud, so keep at it!

You have lived a life that mattered. You have touched thousands of students' lives—some in ways you never imagined. Your lessons may be repeated at work, at play, and in the homes of thousands of former students for decades to come. You have planted seeds of confidence, courage, and curiosity in young minds, who, in their own ways, will make the world a better place. Be proud of that.

You took such good care of yourself throughout your youth; you have now earned the right to become Leonard Cohen. Go ahead—sit in the sun all day, stop exercising, smoke clove cigarettes, and drink champagne first thing in the morning . . . every morning. What are you waiting for?

You have nothing to prove. You never did. The legend of your old age is not in what you accomplish now but in how fully you savor these years. Bring on the chocolate.

Cherish your memories, for they are the footprints of a life well lived. Remember the laughter of your children as they ran through sprinklers in the summer sun, the way their small hands reached for yours in moments of uncertainty. Hold on to the memories of road trips filled with wonder, the times you stood in awe before a breathtaking landscape, and the joy of discovering something new in a place you had never been before. Your travel may have slowed down a bit, but your mind can still wander to those places and relive the joy they brought.

Go through all the boxes of photographs. Watch all the Super 8 movies, the CD videos, and the videos and photos on your phone. Peruse your high school yearbooks. And in between cigarettes and swigs of champagne, throw the tangible evidence of your enchanted life in the trash. No one cares about all that stuff but you, so seal it in whatever remaining space you have in the vault of your memories for you alone. Try with all your might to create new memories, to make others say, "What a pip!"

Find delight in the small things—a perfectly brewed cup of tea, a handwritten letter, and the way light filters through the trees in the late afternoon. Keep learning, even if it's just a new word, a new recipe, or the name of a bird that visits your window. Stay connected to the people who love you, and if they are far, let your words reach them in ways that remind them they are valuable to you.

Let your laughter be a familiar sound, your stories be worth telling, and your heart remain open to wonder. Sing a little each day, always check the back of your hair, yet don't look in rearview mirrors—keep moving forward. Crank the music, dance, and please, no organ recitals . . . "Oh, my liver, my gallbladder, my thyroid, my hanging skin"—keep it to yourself.

Never cease to feel the hum of life around you. Jump into that hum when, how, and if you can. Well, maybe don't jump—step into it. Make it worthwhile that you are still here.

There's a great mystery coming your way, but for now—drink up.
YOUR YOUNGER SELF

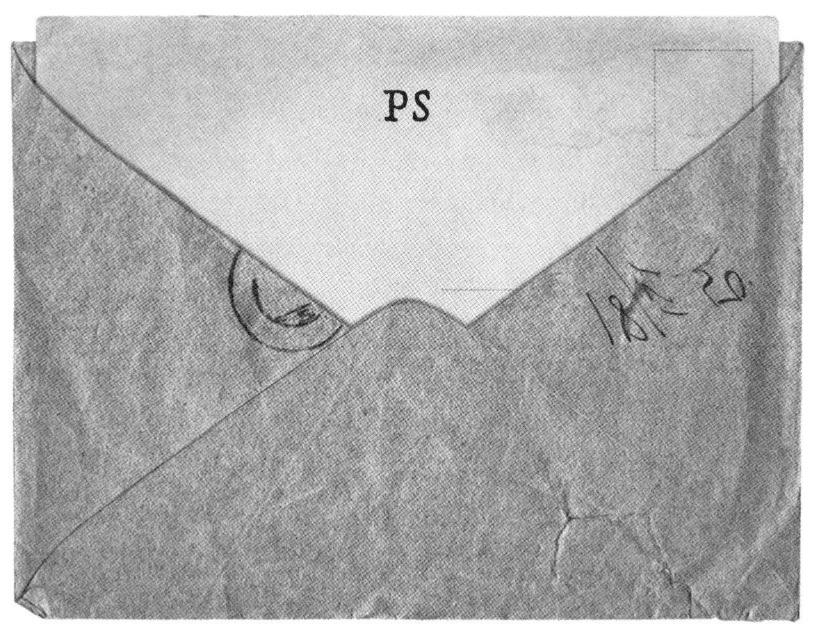
PS

This morning, I drove past a living, breathing, limping embodiment of the purpose of this book.

An elderly gentleman, taking steps gingerly, steadied himself against a purple cane as he made his way to his mailbox. Each shuffle forward was deliberate, each movement a small triumph. I watched as he finally reached his destination, bracing himself before pulling open the metal door.

I did not see what he found there.

But I imagined it.

Bills. Coupons. Voting materials. Insurance cards. Medicare announcements. Maybe an insulting invitation to a seminar on "How to Plan for the Inevitable."

What I did not imagine—but so desperately wanted him to find—was a letter.

No envelope addressed in the familiar loops of an old friend. No ink-smudged words from a grandchild sharing a joke, a triumph, or a secret. No unexpected note that turned an ordinary day into something else—something with warmth, something with memory, or something with love.

I recently saw a human-interest story about a lonely widow who sat each day watching life go by her window. One day, prompted by her isolation, she dropped a handwritten letter in her neighbor's mailbox. The letter simply read, "I live next door. I have no family. I would love to meet you." That was five years ago, and today that widow and her neighbor see each other daily; she has been embraced as a family member. Just a few lines. A hello. An invitation bridging years and loneliness with something so simple yet so rare: a handwritten letter.

This is the last human art form available to all of us.

Writing a letter does not require talent, training, or permission. Just a pen, a moment, and a willingness to reach across time and distance.

I hope these letters have inspired you to write.

Write to someone you love. To someone you wronged. To someone who once made you laugh, or to someone who needs your tears.

Write because it is a small act with a mighty impact.

Write because no one should open an empty mailbox and believe that the world has forgotten them.

Somewhere, someone is waiting for words they don't even know they need—let them find yours.

RONDA

THIS SPACE FOR WRITING MESSAGES

POST CARD

(FOR ADDRESS ONLY)

DEAR DR. BEAMAN,

Your book *A Life in Letters* is a treasure! I have watched your excitement and your struggle as you explored the important ideas and memories that have become this book. I often suggest journaling as a way for clients to decrease depression and reduce anxiety.

Your splendid idea to write letters adds a powerful personal connection. You have gone deeply into feelings of gratitude, disappointment, and distress. By adding the personal connection, you have achieved comfort and compassion. You have grown emotionally and have found peace of mind in the process. Now, with *A Life in Letters*, you have made it possible for others to walk the lively and growth-ful path you have provided.

Warmly,

ALYN BARTICK, LMFT

AIR MAIL ★ POST OFFICE
SPECIAL DELIVERY

Special Delivery

The Healing Power of Letters

Letter writing is a profoundly human act. In this collection, *A Life in Letters*, the personal nature of each letter is evident: These are not simply stories shared or memories recalled but reflections given shape, emotion given form, and love—sometimes messy, complicated, grief-tinged love—put into words. But why letters? Because letter writing holds something unique: a deliberate pause, a chosen audience, and an unspoken hope for connection or release. And as it turns out, this centuries-old practice of addressing someone—real or imagined—has long been recognized as not just meaningful but beneficial to our mental and emotional well-being.

This appendix explores how letter writing contributes to healing, closure, self-awareness, and emotional regulation. It delves into the psychological literature that supports the practice, examines real-world applications, and further encourages you to pick up a pen and use the blank pages in my book not just to remember or honor someone else, but to know and understand yourself more deeply.

Writing as Reflection and Self-Discovery

When you write a letter, especially one that isn't necessarily meant to be sent, you engage in a uniquely introspective act. The practice creates an intentional space for truth telling, for saying the things that are too hard or too complex to speak aloud.

Psychologist James Pennebaker, a leading researcher in expressive writing, has conducted decades of studies showing that writing about emotional experiences can significantly improve both physical and mental health. His work demonstrates that when people write about meaningful, difficult experiences, they often experience reduced stress, better immune function, improved mood, and even fewer visits to the doctor (Pennebaker and Beall 1986). What makes letter writing particularly powerful is that it naturally lends itself to this kind of expressive writing—it has a focus, an audience, and a structure that supports deeper emotional honesty.

Letter writing, especially to someone significant—a parent, partner, child, or even a past version of oneself—allows for a level of clarity and candor that can be both painful and freeing. You're not just recounting events; you're unpacking feelings, motivations, and consequences in a way that helps you understand your own emotional landscape.

Closure, Forgiveness, and Letting Go

Letters can also serve as vessels for closure, especially when communication with someone is no longer possible. Writing to someone who has died, become estranged, or is emotionally unavailable allows the writer to express thoughts and emotions that might otherwise remain unresolved.

A study published in the *Journal of Loss and Trauma* found that writing unsent letters to deceased loved ones helped participants process grief, express unresolved emotions, and find meaning in their loss (Stroebe, Schut, and

Boerner 2017). In bereavement counseling and hospice care, letter writing is frequently used to facilitate a sense of connection and resolution.

Forgiveness, too, can be nurtured through letters. In therapeutic settings, clients are sometimes encouraged to write letters of forgiveness—not necessarily to send but to articulate the pain and the process of letting it go. These letters help externalize and reframe the emotional injury, making space for healing. This approach has been shown to reduce symptoms of depression and anxiety while promoting self-compassion (Witvliet et al. 2002).

Mental Health and Emotional Regulation

In cognitive behavioral therapy (CBT) and other psychological interventions, expressive writing and letter writing are used as tools to help clients reframe negative thinking and develop healthier coping strategies.

According to a 2013 study in *Psychological Science*, when participants wrote about a personal experience from a third-person perspective—as is often done in a letter—they were more likely to demonstrate wisdom-related reasoning, including recognizing the limits of their knowledge and considering others' perspectives (Grossmann and Kross 2014). This distancing can help regulate intense emotions and promote more balanced thinking.

Additionally, writing letters to parts of the self helps people acknowledge internal conflicts and practice self-compassion. Whether it's writing to your younger self, your future self, or a part of yourself that feels broken, the act of naming and addressing those parts with care can be deeply healing.

Connection in a Disconnected Age

In an era dominated by quick texts, comment threads, and fleeting digital interactions, letter writing offers a rare depth. It's intimate. It's slow. It requires attention and intention. Even when a letter is never sent, it feels relational because you are addressing another person or presence.

This sense of imagined or remembered connection is not trivial—it's central to why writing letters feels so therapeutic. Humans are wired for relationship, and letter writing simulates one, providing a container for what psychologist Donald Winnicott called the "transitional space"—a safe place between you and another where emotion and imagination meet.

Letter Writing in Practice

The applications of therapeutic letter writing are as varied as the human experiences that inspire them:

- **Letters to the dead** can help grievers find words for their loss and feel ongoing bonds with those they've lost.
- **Letters of gratitude** have been shown to increase happiness and decrease depressive symptoms (Seligman et al. 2005).
- **Anger letters**—where you write out unfiltered rage—can be cathartic, especially when followed by reflection or reframing.
- **Letters from the future** (e.g., "Dear Me in Ten Years") can boost hope and goal setting.
- **Letters never meant to be sent** give voice to the unspeakable, offering a pressure release without real-world consequences.

Why It Belongs in This Book

A Life in Letters was never meant to be just a personal project. It was always, quietly, an invitation—for others to reflect, to write, to say the things they never got to say. If you find yourself holding on to a memory, a regret, an unshed tear or an unspoken thank-you, you might find relief and revelation in writing a letter.

You don't have to be a writer. You only have to be honest. Start with "Dear . . ." and see what follows.

Some letters will surprise you with their rage. Others may come out as poems. Some may make you cry in public, and some may lighten you so much you float. They may be addressed to people you love, people you've lost, people you miss, or people you need to release. Some may be to yourself.

Let them be messy. Let them be unfinished. Let them be yours.

Getting Started: A Few Prompts to Fill the Blank Page

- Write a letter to someone who hurt you but you're still thinking about.
- Write to someone who's no longer living and tell them what you wish you had said.
- Write a letter from your younger self to who you are now.
- Write a letter to a future version of yourself.
- Write a thank-you letter to someone who shaped you.
- Write to a version of yourself that survived something hard.

Conclusion: The Letter as Legacy

A letter is more than words on a page. It is a witness. A testimony. A small, contained act of bravery. Whether shared or sealed in a drawer, it says, "This mattered. I mattered. You mattered."

In the act of writing, we tether ourselves to our truths. We release our ghosts. We remember we are not alone. And perhaps most beautifully, we leave behind not just a record of our thoughts but a trail of our becoming ever more deeply and beautifully human.

Selected References

Grossmann, I., and E. Kross. 2014. "Exploring Solomon's Paradox: Self-Distancing Eliminates the Self-Other Asymmetry in Wise Reasoning about Close Relationships in Younger and Older Adults." *Psychological Science* 25 (8): 1571–1580.

Pennebaker, J. W., and S. K. Beall. 1986. "Confronting a Traumatic Event: Toward an Understanding of Inhibition and Disease. *Journal of Abnormal Psychology* 95 (3): 274–281.

Seligman, M. E. P., T. A. Steen, N. Park, and C. Peterson. 2005. "Positive Psychology Progress: Empirical Validation of Interventions." *American Psychologist* 60 (5): 410–421.

Stroebe, M., H. Schut, and K. Boerner. 2017. "Cautioning Health-Care Professionals: Bereaved Persons Are Misguided Through the Stages of Grief." *Omega: Journal of Death and Dying* 74 (4): 455–473.

Witvliet, C. V. O., T. E. Ludwig, and K. L. Vander Laan. 2002. "Granting Forgiveness or Harboring Grudges: Implications for Emotion, Physiology, and Health." *Psychological Science* 12 (2): 117–123.

Letter Doula

In the tapestry of human connection, words serve as the threads that weave our stories, emotions, and legacies together. Yet articulating our deepest sentiment—be it love, gratitude, or farewell—can often be a daunting endeavor. This is where the compassion and experience of a letter doula become invaluable, guiding individuals through the intimate process of letter writing with empathy and expertise.

Letter Doula—Bring Your Letters to Life

As a letter doula, I will be more than just a writing assistant; I am your companion on your journey to self-expression. My mission is to help illustrate your letter's intention in a way that reads uniquely *you*. Whether you're penning a legacy letter, a heartfelt apology, or words of encouragement, I ensure your message resonates authentically.

The Multifaceted Benefits of Engaging Letter Doula

1. **Emotional support:** Writing significant letters can evoke a spectrum of emotions. Letter Doula offers a safe space to explore these feelings, providing empathy and encouragement throughout the process.
2. **Expert guidance:** With expertise in writing and storytelling, Letter Doula assists in structuring your letter, choosing the right words, and ensuring clarity and coherence in conveying your message.
3. **Facilitated reflection:** Delving into personal memories and values can be challenging. Letter Doula facilitates this introspection, helping you uncover and articulate the sentiments you wish to express.
4. **Personalized approach:** Recognizing that every individual's story is unique, Letter Doula tailors each letter to align with your personality, values, and the specific purpose of your letter.
5. **Legacy creation:** Beyond crafting a letter, Letter Doula contributes to the creation of a meaningful legacy, ensuring your words endure and resonate with recipients long after they are written.

Why Choose Letter Doula?

At Letter Doula, the commitment to honoring your voice and story is paramount. By reaching out, you can take the first step toward your perfect letter. Whether you'd like to create a farewell letter, a letter of advice, or a memoir, Letter Doula is dedicated to bringing your letters to life with care and purpose.

Connect with Letter Doula

Embarking on the journey of meaningful letter writing is a profound endeavor, and you don't have to navigate it alone. Contact Letter Doula today to experience the transformative power of guided self-expression.

LetterDoula.com
(805) 500-3755

In a world where digital communication often lacks depth,
rediscover the timeless art of letter writing with the
compassionate guidance of Letter Doula.
Your words have the power to heal, connect, and leave a lasting legacy.
Let Letter Doula help you bring them to life.

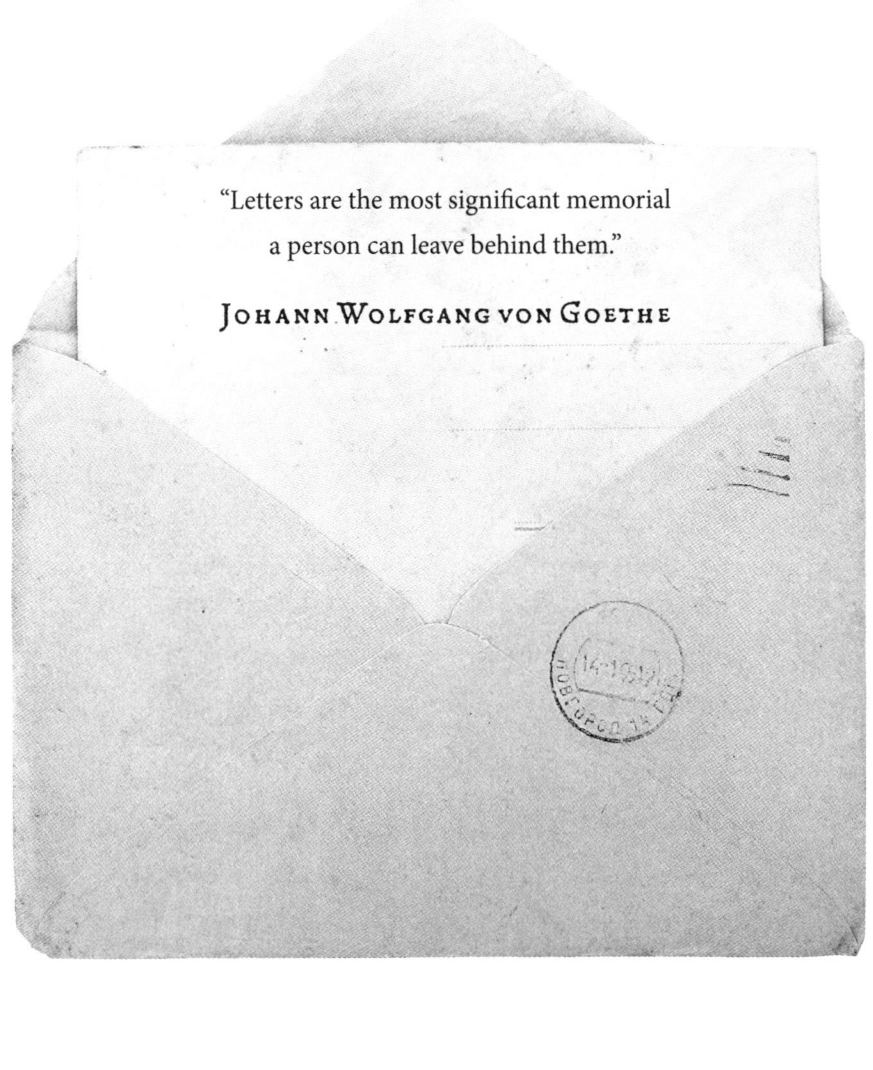
"Letters are the most significant memorial
a person can leave behind them."
Johann Wolfgang von Goethe

For inquiries regarding speaking engagements,
workshops and book club/bookstore appearances
contact Dr. Beaman at **ronda@peaklearning.com.**

About the Author

Dr. Ronda Beaman is an award-winning educator, bestselling author, executive coach, and nationally recognized speaker whose work centers on leadership, resilience, and creative expression.

As the chief creative officer of PEAK Learning, Inc., and clinical professor of leadership at California Polytechnic University, Ronda has empowered thousands to find their voices—in the classroom, the boardroom, and now, on the page.

Named the first recipient of the National Education Association's Art of Teaching award, she is known for her irreverent humor, raw honesty, and deep compassion. Her previous books include *Little Miss Merit Badge*, *You're Only Young Twice*, and the bestselling *My Feats in These Shoes*.

With *A Life in Letters*, Ronda invites readers to rediscover one of the last human arts: writing with intention, vulnerability, and heart. When she's not teaching or coaching, you'll find her writing actual letters (with stamps!), hosting workshops, or helping others find their voices through writing.

She lives in San Luis Obispo, California, and online at letterdoula.com.